THE DEBT FREE SCREAM

*How We Paid Off $175,000
Of Student Loans In 30 Months*

THE DEBT FREE SCREAM
Copyright © 2018 by Jeanna Infantino

THE DEBT FREE SCREAM

How We Paid Off $175,000
Of Student Loans In 30 Months

JEANNA INFANTINO

TABLE OF CONTENTS

INTRODUCTION

This book is written to give you hope if you're like the rest of the 44 million of us with 1.3 trillion dollars in student loan debt. It's written to show you that if I can do it, you can do it too. My husband and I paid off over $175,000 in student loan debt in thirty months. During those months we got engaged, had our dream wedding, went on the honeymoon of a lifetime to Sri Lanka and the Maldives, bought a car(s), went on numerous trips, attended more weddings than I can count, moved twice (maybe three times, but who's counting), adopted a dog, experienced many of life's unexpected events, and were still able to live a fulfilling and exciting life. The point is, that while we were strict with our finances, living off of 39 percent of our monthly net income, we were still able to enjoy our day to day living and then some.

I've always been conscious of money. What things cost, how much I'm saving, and if I really need that new pair of shoes. I didn't imagine a life where money would be an issue and that I would one day be in debt—serious, overwhelming, how-are-we-going-to-get-out-of-this debt.

I, like you, went to a four-year college where I succumbed to the private tuition that cost my parents and I an arm, a leg, and really all of our other limbs. We accepted the norm of $48,000 PER YEAR for school because that's how our society works. $48,000 for school, PER YEAR, sure. $10,000 for a meal plan, sure. $15,000 for student housing, sure. $150k+ for a college education, SURE. Bring. It. On. A college education is one expense that we don't question in the United States. The fact that at eighteen years old you can start signing away over $100k in loans is a bit crazy. In reality, an eighteen-year-old might have better luck buying a house for the same price and investing in their future in less conventional ways. I was lucky in the fact that my parents helped pay for a large amount of my tuition. I was able to graduate a semester early to cut on costs, I worked a part-time job when I was home on vacation, and lived minimally during my four years in college. Lucky for you, we'll get into more detail on minimalist living later.

The fact of the matter is that we spend twelve years of our lives preparing to get into college. Unfortunately, it's rare that anyone prepares us for the financial burden that typically accompanies college. This education could be the difference between financial freedom and an eternity of student loan payments. This is where we need to do better for ourselves, our children, and ultimately the future of our country. Gaining some foundational knowledge in personal finance can help you both eliminate your student loans and prevent future financial hardships. No longer will you play the victim or use the words "bad luck." Not living paycheck to paycheck will be a wonderful feeling!

How I Got Here

You can say that the real debt, the one that made me write this book, was one that I was "grandfathered" into. I had my fair share of student loan debt, but it was nothing compared to what my husband had accumulated. I like to refer to anything over $150,000 as "Massive Debt." My husband, who was at that time my boyfriend, and I moved to Baltimore after undergrad where he would spend three years earning his doctorate in physical therapy.

In total, he had seven years of growing college loans that were astronomical. This was on top of my undergrad loans which, in the grand scheme of things, were just a hair of his loan debt. Prior to starting graduate school he already had nearly $100k in student loans. He didn't go to a private school which begged the question of how and why he had so many private loans. His college education should have been manageable: $40k at most for a 4-year public New York State University. However, this was not the case.

Looking back, I vividly remember when he would receive a check for the balance of his loan. He would use it to eat out for the week or go buy a new pair of sneakers—all with a portion of his student loan. To him, it was money that was left over from his tuition so he was going to enjoy it! He wasn't thinking about having to pay back the extra $5,000 plus the 9 percent interest on top of that. I use this as an example because in college we are still kids. We didn't know that $5,000 here and there actually ends up turning into $100k later on down the road. Unless you had the opportunity to take a very in-depth finance class in high school, then it's likely that you fell into this category also. Ignorance is not always bliss and what we don't know eventually hurts us. Not being informed is just one way that many of these private loan companies can take advantage of students. We were a living example of how to use loans carelessly. Therefore, we had to suffer the consequences of those decisions.

When grad school came around we weren't falling into those same traps. We decided to only take out the bare minimum of what was needed to pay for tuition each semester. Living expenses would be paid for by income and no longer loans. Tuition fees would be the only thing growing our debt. It wouldn't be a penny more than what the semester cost. Over the next few years, I would continue working two jobs, my full-time job and waitressing on the side. My husband Michael continued working towards his doctorate and got as many side jobs on campus as he could handle. By doing this, we were able to cover rent, food, and the usual expenses without having to take out additional loans. It's safe to say this helped, but we learned a little too late.

When Michael was a month from graduating and officially becoming a doctor of physical therapy, we knew it was time to get the numbers in line and actually see what the damage was. We were aware that he had undergrad loans, private loans, graduate loans, etc. When we finally had consolidated all of the loan totals, I wasn't prepared for the number that was staring back at us. Do you know how much seven years' worth of a non-private college costs? I do. $172,000. Before interest.

I didn't study finance in school as a communications major and Michael obviously studied sciences. We weren't going to be bringing in the big bucks upon graduating, we knew that. We came to the realization that this giant debt could be a life game changer; if we figured it out or if we didn't. At that moment we had to decide if we were going to knock out our debt as fast as possible or do the standard fifteen- to twenty-year repayment plan. Potentially racking up an additional $60-100k in interest alone. We chose to tackle it head on! Helmet, cleats, and shoulder pads; we were committed and started to make a plan.

My Story in a Nutshell

Before I dive right in, I'll give you a quick snapshot of who I am and the last 27 years of my life. I was born and raised in typical small town USA in the Catskills in upstate New York with my sister and parents. My parents were born there, built a house, and haven't left since. Much of what I know about money I learned from their own practices. Of course, at the time we didn't actually have conversations about money, but they unknowingly set the example for how to responsibly handle money. Growing up, we certainly were not rich, but we weren't poor either. My parents were extremely generous and I always felt I had everything I wanted. However, it's important to know that we weren't vacationing in Majorca, Spain or living in a 5,000 sq. ft. house. We were perfectly comfortable. Summer vacations were to the Jersey Shore, my mom drove us around in a giant Astro van, we played outside in the homemade fort and teepee my dad built us, and our clothes were purchased at JCPenney and Old Navy. It was the perfect life growing up in the 90s.

My mom and dad are still the hardest working people I know. They do not know how to relax nor how to spend a weekend doing nothing. My dad is an auto mechanic who ended up purchasing the garage he worked at from the time he was sixteen years old. My mom is the "boss" in dad's office and has an additional job at our local town building. As for spending, my mom was never one to spend money on herself and my dad's largest purchases came down to anything with four wheels. Tractors, trailers, ATVs, you name it. They never spent more money than they were making and although they rarely told us no, they were not afraid to. My parents never had a debit card or used an ATM machine. When I first opened my own bank account I didn't know how easy it was to access money. Put in your code and voila! Money is spitting out at your fingertips. Their practices influenced my behavior from the time I knew what money even was. As a child, I remember being very concerned with money and what things cost. I never wanted my parents to spend too much on me and I didn't ask for expensive things. Any time I received money as a gift for Christmas or my birthday I would save it. I didn't want to spend a single dollar. Fast forward to today and my parents still criticize me for being "cheap." I like to call it money conscious. It's clear that money was always in the forefront of my mind and I understood that my parents worked hard for all that they gave to my sister and me.

At age sixteen, I started working. I dove right into working two jobs and continued that for the next eight years. My first jobs were a snowboard instructor by day and bussing tables by night. They were only a mile from each other so I was able to maximize my time and make more money. Over the next few years in high school I had various waitressing, babysitting, and random bartending jobs. I was always open to the next opportunity that would put more cash in my pocket. In retrospect, I was never saving for anything specific; I just liked seeing my bank account grow. College happened and I spent the next four years working during summer vacations. Making as much money as possible to help fund my college expenses while at school. Fast forward. After earning a college degree and making a big move to Maryland, I was desperately searching for a job to start paying off my school loans. Less than a week after moving to Baltimore, I started waitressing at a restaurant in the Inner Harbor while interviewing for a job that I hoped to make a career. I was loving the quick cash I was making as a waitress. When I accepted a job offer at a Hilton Hotel I wasn't ready to relinquish my waitressing job. Three years later, I decided to quit waitressing as I moved up the ladder in the Events Departments at the Hilton. As much as I loved the easy money it was hard to balance both jobs. Looking back, I am amazed that I lasted for three years working multiple jobs. Fast forward three more years and a few promotions, I am continuing my career at the Hilton after transitioning from the Assistant Director of Events to a Sales Manager. From here, the future awaits.

Chapter 1:
Our Introduction to Dave Ramsey

There's no hidden secret or quick fix to getting out of debt. You commit, you make sacrifices, you plan, and you just do it. Our life changed when we were introduced to a financial mogul who in the world of debt is much like a celebrity: Dave Ramsey. I often refer to Dave Ramsey as if I know him on a personal level and we're BFFs. Interestingly enough, many people aren't familiar with him and his system for living a debt-free life. He has an entire program focused on getting out of debt and accumulating wealth. Real wealth, not get rich quick schemes. This program is called *Financial Peace*. If I were to list the steps to getting out of debt it would start with this:

Step 1: Research Dave Ramsey and his program *Financial Peace*. Every other step will fall into place after.

We were set up with our own financial advisor who would coach us over the next few weeks on our expenses and how to budget. They provide you with the initial tools and understanding on how to plan and make your own personalized budget. After you're set up for success, the rest is up to you alone.

Following our conversations with our financial advisor, we began tracking our expenses to determine what a realistic monthly budget for our daily living would look like. To track your expenses you have to keep track of every penny and dollar spent. It can be on something as small as a bottle of water at the convenience store and as large as a new engine for your car. Track everything. Once the day-to-day budget was set we then had to determine our annual or "periodic" spending. This is money spent throughout the year. Periodic refers to annual spending or things that are yearly occurrences. These can also be labeled as "buckets" that you might be saving up for. This will include items such as gifts, travel, car insurance, home repairs, and medical expenses. You can imagine periodic spending to include "unforeseen" expenses that you may not have planned for. The great thing is that you're still always prepared for them because you have them in your budget.

Once you have a budget, you no longer feel as if you're doing something wrong by spending money because each "bucket" of expenses is allotted for. For example, if you give yourself $200 a month for dining out then you don't need to feel guilty when you use that money to indulge in something like a great sushi dinner. This bucket would be your restaurant bucket. It's important to choose where your money goes based on what's important to you. If you know that entertainment is your thing then create a budget for it. If you know that you like to watch TV and want to watch *The Bachelor* every Monday night, budget for it. The point is to choose a budget that is realistic for you as an individual so that you can stick with it. You wouldn't set goals that you couldn't meet, so why set a budget that would be impossible to maintain?

One of my important buckets when creating our budget was travel. I'm not someone who likes to buy "stuff" or get the latest Amazon deal of the day. However, I do like to indulge in a good vacation, whether it be a weekend trip to Virginia or an entire weeks' vacation to the beach. In the last couple of years, Michael and I have been able to travel more than ever by taking advantage of our resources and incorporating it into our budget. We often get asked how we're able to travel so much and still live life on a budget. The short answer is that we choose what's important to us and put our money in areas that are meaningful to us. You could choose to put that money elsewhere or you could put it straight towards loans. It's all based on what works for you and what's important for maintaining your lifestyle.

"Change is painful. Few people have the courage to seek out change. Most people won't change until the pain of where they are exceeds the pain of change."

— Dave Ramsey, The Total Money Makeover: Classic Edition: A Proven Plan for Financial Fitness

Comfortably, Uncomfortable: Questioning Societal Norms

Living a life on a budget isn't meant to restrict you, but rather to give you the freedom to do what you want to do in a responsible manner. People who have the self-control, self-confidence, and determination to pay off their debt will be the ones to succeed. Those are all characteristics that I would like to portray, wouldn't you? You'll come to the realization that you don't need the latest iPhone and would rather stay in and cook instead of spending $50 out at a restaurant. You might choose to keep your 2002 car that's still holding strong at 150,000 miles and save an extra $10,000. Who cares what others are driving around town? They're most likely in debt and their car is probably a lease.

To make this work, you might have to change your mindset. Just slightly. Our culture is based on always wanting more. You know it, you live here too. It's having it all to keep up with the rest of society when, in reality, the majority of Americans are struggling to pay their own home mortgage. Sixty years ago, the average American's debt was just under $4,000. Today, it's $137,063! This is a compilation of credit card debt, mortgages, car(s), and student loans. (https://www.daveramsey.com/blog/5-money-problems-didnt-have-50-years-ago?ictid=aw15)

The biggest hurdle you might face is getting away from what you know and changing how you've lived for the past twenty, thirty, or forty years. You want to embrace this journey of becoming debt free. You're making a plan for your life and there is certainly no negative connotation to that. Your family and friends might not support your lifestyle changes right away, but don't let that stop you. It's important to not worry about what other people think. This is your life and your future. Once you start experiencing the possibilities of no longer living in debt, I promise that you'll feel motivated. You might, like myself, want to share your experiences with everyone you know so that it provides them with hope. I'm not here to preach on how to save money, but to give hope and to tell you that if you have a plan and know where your money is going, then becoming debt free really is that simple.

Don't Be Influenced, Be an Influencer

We all know that the people who you surround yourself with will influence your life. Take a look at your circle of family and friends and those who are closest to you. Ask yourself if they're affecting your ability to make this plan work. If they are, you need to have the confidence to be different. This may sound easier than it actually is, but if you don't have the confidence in yourself then you will succumb to their influences. Often times these influences are in relation to money and how it's spent. For example, you go out with your friends and everyone is spending $100 per person at a restaurant. You need the confidence to be okay with the fact that you're only going to choose to spend $30. Will you hear comments from the peanut gallery? Maybe. Should you care? No. Always have your end goal in mind and you'll be just fine with passing on the filet and ordering a juicy burger. Lastly, do it proudly! At times you might have to just say no to a night out or decline a wedding invite from a friend from college. These are the situations that you'll come across and find it's not easy to say no. However, these are also the types of situations that can save you an exorbitant amount of money each time. It's a known fact that not everyone can attend every birthday, wedding, and holiday, so don't sweat it. In time, you'll be able to do all that you want and to the greatest extent.

Throughout the book, I have compiled some easy tips listed as "My 2 Cents" that I have found to be beneficial throughout our debt-free journey. You'll see those placed throughout the chapters in random order.

My 2 Cents #1
Don't get wrapped up in the ease of meals sent to your door, clothes picked out for you, fitness in a box, snacks in a box, dog treats in a box. It's all TOO MUCH!

Find that Support System: Suffering Together is Better than Suffering Alone

Like with any team setting, you always do better when you have support and someone to share your experiences with. If you can find a friend or family member that wants to become debt free it will greatly benefit you. Having any support system when you're making life changes is always helpful. It'll allow you to share stories and motivate one another as you navigate through some of your experiences. If you find that you're having trouble making decisions on certain aspects of your plan, talk them out. Use that relationship to coach one another and share some of the things that you've found to work in your plan. We have many friends that were in the same situation as us with massive debt upon graduating. One of our good friends decided to follow the *Financial Peace* program at the same time that we were. This helped us out because we could share the same experiences with them and enjoy our time together without spending money. We all had a common goal and it allowed us to put ourselves in situations that helped us achieve our goals rather than hinder them. Our aunt and uncle were also great examples for us as they were living proof that the system works. In fact, they are the ones that introduced us to Dave Ramsey from the start. We were able to not only see their successes and how they manage their money, but also how they give their money to the church, organizations that are important to them, and those in need.

It's possible that you don't know anyone that wants to take on the challenge and become debt free. Don't limit yourself by only looking in your circle. The church is also a great resource and most provide groups and additional options to learn about *Financial Peace*. There is often a leader that manages the program and they'll meet on a weekly basis. Those that attend can be your own support system and give you the extra motivation needed to stay committed.

For us as a couple, there were a few challenges that we had to overcome early on. While I was always money conscious, my other half was not. We had to find a balance and commit to seeing this through together. There are always two ends of the spectrum and it's important to meet in the middle to ensure this works. You'll find what each of your needs are and what you're not willing to budge on. You'll see your communication skills as a couple improve and you'll learn how to compromise with the value of giving and taking. However, it also means that you need to rely on someone else and their choices. If you are single, you have to hold yourself accountable since you get to make the choices on your own. If you're in a relationship or marriage then it's imperative that both of you are on board with becoming debt free. I promise you that if only 50 percent of your household is following the budget then you are 100 percent guaranteed to fail. Not to mention that there will be some frustrating arguments in your future over purchases made. Michael will tell you that at some points he was afraid to buy things as inexpensive as a sandwich because he didn't want to have to log it into the sacred spreadsheet. We also had to adjust to the fact that we couldn't live a life as if we were debt free.

A great quote that you'll hear from Dave Ramsey is, "Live like no one else, so you can live like no one else." We would often remind each other of this quote when we wanted to do something or make a purchase that wasn't in the budget. It became a fun way to hold ourselves accountable and make good choices. There would be no more buying drinks for the group at the bar and covering tabs. There would be no more $100 trips to Target out of boredom. I know I sound harsh. I sound like the bad guy who doesn't want to have any fun. But guess what? We worked it out quickly and because of those little daily changes, we're living a life free of debt after just thirty months. I give you these short stories throughout this book because I want you to know that it won't all be easy. Keep yourselves motivated together and celebrate your milestones. Before long you too will be doing the Debt Free Scream.

CHAPTER 2:
HOW WE MADE OUR BUDGET

"A budget is people telling their money where to go instead of wondering where it went."

— Dave Ramsey, The Total Money Makeover:
Classic Edition: A Proven Plan for Financial Fitness

When most people hear the word budget they associate it with a negative connotation. You might think that it's putting yourself on a restriction to things that you can no longer have; similar to when you hear the word diet. In reality, a budget allows a person to plan for what they're spending and, in some ways, gives the individual freedom to spend more. It's taking a step back to look at what you're currently doing and find ways to change bad spending habits. Throughout this book, you'll hear me use the word "plan" very often. Budgeting creates a plan for your future. It allows you to plan for each item or category that you're spending on so that you can stay within a set budget. We used a seven-step plan from Dave Ramsey as our guideline throughout this process. Much of this book is based on Step 2 alone. The other steps may come later in life, possibly ten to fifteen years later, but as long as you follow this plan you'll see great outcomes. (https://www.daveramsey.com/baby-steps)

Step 1: Save $1,000 cash in an emergency fund
Step 2: Use the debt snowball to pay off all your debt (except your house)
Step 3: A fully funded emergency fund of three to six months of expenses

Step 4: Invest 15 percent of your household income into retirement
Step 5: Start saving for college
Step 6: Pay off your home early
Step 7: Build wealth and give generously

Building Our Emergency Fund

The first step in creating a budget is looking at your finances to see how much money you have in savings. You always want to have enough for an emergency fund in case something comes up. The emergency fund amount can vary based on what stage of life you're in. Take into account factors like a steady job, if you have dual income, if you have children, etc. When you're in debt you want as much money as possible to go toward loan payments. The emergency fund at this point if you have a steady job and no kids would be $1,000. Enough so that if you have a real emergency you can manage. You might ask yourself what qualifies as an emergency. I would categorize the following as emergencies: health-related illness, a broken down car, or no heat in the dead of winter. If it's something that inhibits your day to day living, then it's likely an emergency. Once you are debt free, this emergency fund will grow and become three to six months of living expenses, but let's take this one step at a time.

Tracking Your Spending

When first establishing your budget, you'll want to track all of your spending for one month to see what a realistic budget will look like for you. I used an Excel document that became my best friend over the last two-and-a-half years. I would track every dollar spent by month and also by day. Set up a document first by month and then make columns for each day of the month. From there, you'll have rows of expenses or what we call line items. Examples of monthly line items include the following: groceries, gas, restaurants, rent, cable, entertainment, utilities, etc. Each time you go to the store or get gas, save that receipt and enter it into the correct day of the month. It's amazing how doing this holds you accountable for the money that you spend. When you can visualize how much money you are spending on each item it puts it into greater perspective. It makes you question what you actually need versus what you want. An example of a simplified spreadsheet is below. The numbers in parentheses are negatives, showing we have gone over budget in that category. If you find yourself going over budget in the same category each month, re-evaluate that category.

January

	Current Month Cash Balance	Day 1	Day 2	Day 3	Day 4	Day 5
Groceries	($58.55)		$89.20		$102.25	
Restaurants	$173.81			$26.19		
Fuel/ Transportation	$141.51	$32.99				$25.50
Cell Phone	$0	$181.00				

February

	Current Month Cash Balance	Day 1	Day 2	Day 3	Day 4	Day 5
Groceries	$107.25	$75.50			$42.25	
Restaurants	$134.95	$52.45				$12.60
Fuel/ Transportation	$166		$34.00			
Cell Phone	$0	$181.00				

Re-Evaluating Our Budget

After your first thirty days of tracking your spending, you can see what totals you have in each category. From there you can then figure out how much you can cut out, even if it's just $50 a month. You want to make a budget that is feasible, but also challenging so that you are saving money and not living paycheck to paycheck. If you notice that you are spending an exorbitant amount on eating out, then that would be something to reevaluate. Your $200 a month allotted food budget could get cut back to $150 a month. If you're feeling really strong and want to push yourself further, cut back to $100 a month. It's a budget, it's not supposed to be easy. If your grocery budget is $250 a month, think of creative ways to reduce it and look at what you're eating. I like to make weekly meal plans to see what I'm going to cook for the week. This ensures that I use all of the food I have purchased so that I'm not wasteful. Subbing out meat for vegetables can save a great deal of money every week. Stir fry, chili, and soups are some of my favorites and the best part is that they last for days! Three things I live by in my weekly plan: leftovers, breakfast for dinner once a week, and limit the amount of meat I purchase. You can easily save $80 a month by doing so.

My 2 Cents #2

Buy when items are on sale and don't buy out of season. You'll spend triple the amount. This applies to food items, not clothing. This is truest when buying fruit and vegetables. You'll start noticing when items are in season because they become heavily discounted. For example, I refuse to buy grapes out of season because they'll cost $7 a bag. When in season, I can get them for half the price. Avocados are another item that can only be purchased in season. If you're spending $2.50 per avocado, then you need to keep reading.

Non-Negotiable Items

There are obviously line items that are non-negotiable to cut back on. Gas is an essential expense, but you can sometimes earn discounts by using grocery store points. If you're driving to work daily, just keep track of your spending so that it's accurate for the month. Utilities are another essential, but be cognizant of turning off lights, water usage, etc. Those are easy ways to save a few dollars each month. One personal example that saved me $75 a month ($900 a year) was cutting back on our cable bill. The internet is a necessity for us, but 150 channels and a DVR was not. We reevaluated what we were paying monthly for cable and decided that $160 a month to watch television wasn't worth it. To be honest, I watch two channels so I was going to find other ways to watch my Bravo and HGTV shows. Hence, the internet, Netflix, the Fire Stick, and the Apple TV that we had. It's 2018 and cable is no longer the only option. Continue to take a look at each of your expenses and get creative where you can cut back. Make it a challenge!

My 2 Cents #3
Stop paying for that $150/month gym membership. I know this one might be hard if you're dedicated to CrossFit, yoga or Orange Theory. I get it, you want to be healthy, but there are other ways for less than $1,800 a year.

Finding Ways to Trim the Fat

Have you ever heard the saying "live below your means?" This is 100 percent true. If you're serious about paying off your debt and doing it quickly you just need to live by those four words. Every decision you make should come back to this. Do you really need that brand new 2018 SUV? Do you need that two-bedroom apartment that comes with not only a pool, but that movie theater with free popcorn? The answer is almost always going to be a no.

Housing was always our largest monthly expense and I was determined to keep that within a reasonable budget. Deciding to move out of the city allowed us to save $1,000 a month in rent. This is huge, which is why I urge you to first look at your living situation. For me, there were things that I was willing to sacrifice and others that I wasn't. We knew our needs and wants and found a place that worked for us. Needs for me were a washer/dryer unit in my apartment, natural light, location, free parking, and a gym. For some, the gym may not be a need, but if my husband and I were each to buy a gym membership, that would be an additional $1,500 to $2,000 per year. I'll take it with my apartment instead. Your need list might be completely different. You might want granite countertops or hardwood floors. Maybe an outdoor patio. These are all things that you can still have. Remember to keep in mind what works for you as an individual because all of our needs are not the same.

If you find that you are heavily undercutting your budget and spending much less, tighten it up where you can. The more you save, the faster those loans get paid off. Having approximately $3,000 left over each month to put toward student loans felt great! Once you begin to see the loans dwindle it'll give you more motivation. You'll want to pay them off even faster and put every spare dollar towards the balance.

My 2 Cents #4

Use the internet or DVDs to find a killer workout. There are so many great ways aside from paying for a gym membership to still get the same effect.

Periodic Budget: Planning for the Year

I briefly mentioned a periodic budget and how that works. Remember, periodics can also be labeled as "buckets" that you might be saving up for. When planning our wedding we had a periodic fund and our goal was our wedding budget. If you're saving for a house deposit that would be periodic. Others include travel, gifts, car repairs, clothing, subscriptions, pet insurance, etc. You want to plan for these on a yearly budget since they may not occur each month. For example, if you want to allocate $200 per year towards clothing, you would divide that by twelve months, making your monthly clothing periodic just $16.66. Each month you won't actually be spending $16.66, but it will be coming out of your monthly cash flow so that you have it saved when needed. If you want to save $6,000 for a wedding, divide it by twelve months and allocate $500 a month toward it.

After listing all periodic categories, you'll add up your periodic totals for the year and divide it by twelve months. This will give you your monthly periodic sum, which will be added to each month's expenses. You'll go through and do this exercise with each of your periodic categories once each year. The great part is that when it comes time to buy a new pair of shoes you've already budgeted and will have that money in your savings.

Keep in mind that periodic spending can be a large amount, depending on what you have going on in your life at that time.

For me, periodic sums are one area where I feel I can cut back and save more money. I have a large amount coming out each month ($1,300 to be exact) to be used for various large expenses throughout the year. This means that I have $15,600 for the year to be used for travel, gifts, insurance, medical expenses, home repairs, pet care, etc. It does indeed sound like a lot of money that could be used towards loans. However, one of the greater lessons that I've learned is that you don't want to find yourself in a situation where you don't have the money to pay for something as important as a medical expense, should it arise. The great thing is that if you have leftover periodic money at the end of the year you can throw an extra $2,000 towards your loan for that month.

We were able to save a significant amount of money for our wedding in eighteen months by using this budget plan. When determining a budget for all weeks, months, and years you'll always want to work backward. For our wedding, I worked backward to determine how much money I wanted to have saved by the date of our wedding. From there I divided it by the number of months to figure out how much needed to come out of each month's income to make sure we reached our number. You'll want to do the same thing for each individual bucket. When we started sending in deposits for our wedding, we already had a fund designated so it never felt like we were in a money pit. The money was accounted for and I knew what my budget was for each item.

It's extremely important to be specific when planning for both your monthly budget and your periodic budget. It can be easy to get lost in the world of estimates. The challenge with estimating is that it can put you thousands of dollars over or under your budget. Take the time to go through each line item in detail to make sure that it's accurate. More importantly, when tracking your expenses you have to be 100 percent specific. If you overdrew in an area or have leftover money, you may have messed up somewhere along the way. It may take a few months to get it right, but you have to find constancy. In the first few months don't be afraid to tweak your budget to make it fit what you can do. That constancy will engrain habits in yourself and make this a subconscious process in no time at all. Below is an example of our periodic budget, but this is just one option for how you can track. If there is another way that you want to track your monthly spending, try it. There's no right or wrong way to create your own spreadsheets. Each year we continue to tweak ours to make it more accurate; we add comments to what we spent and have a column showing what we have left at the end of each month.

My 2 Cents #5

When planning a wedding, absolutely make sure you set a budget. If you don't have any budget, you'll spend an exorbitant amount of money and you could end up regretting your purchases. Whether it's $5,000 or $30,000, always set a budget.

Periodic Spreadsheet

	A	B	C	D	E
1		TOTAL	August	September	October
2	Car Insurance	1329	1329		
3	Renters Insurance	243	243		
4	Household Fund	200			328
5	Maintenance/Repairs	700	341		17.99
6	Medical Care	200		80	75
7	Dental Care	144			
8	Pharmacy	200			
9	Vision	180			
10	Jeanna BEAUTY	200			
11	Charity	400	185	20	
12	Vacation	4800	450	166.05	50.96
13	Gifts	2500	207	795.96	161
14	Vet Care	500			65
15	Boarding/Grooming	1000	25		52
16	Pet insurance	412.35	412.35		
17	Recreational Activities	700	225	111	20
18	Memberships/Education/Books	600	150		
19	Rehab Renegade	2000	34		
20	Clothing	550	103	15	29
21	EZ PASS	250			
22	**Total Periodics for Year**	17108.35		1188.01	798.95

Tools to Track Your Budget

Setting the budget is the easy part. Once you have a budget you have to commit to tracking all of the items in your budget. Everyone has different ways of tracking, but be mindful of putting your expenses into your spreadsheet on at least a weekly basis. I teetered on the obsessive side of the spectrum and would put my expenses in at the end of each day. I did this to make sure that I didn't forget to track a single dollar. My husband would track them on his phone, waiting until the end of the week to put them in the spreadsheet. Now, there are so many great apps that help make the process easier. **EveryDollar** is an app that allows you to set up your budget and track in real time. The challenge with not making tracking a daily occurrence is that by the time you end up putting the last week or twos' expenses in, you may have already maxed out your budget. Visually seeing the numbers go into the spreadsheet helps with accountability and allows you to see where you are for each line item. At any given time I can tell you how much money we have left in the grocery budget, the restaurant budget, or the entertainment budget. By making this a routine and tracking daily you'll have greater success and will be less likely to go over budget.

Planning for the Month, the Day, the Year

What you might experience, like me, is that at the beginning of each month you'll want to spend all of your money. You have just started a fresh budget and you're feeling rich! You want to buy everything that you have just deprived yourself of for the last few days or weeks. You waited two weeks to go out to a new restaurant you've wanted to try. You waited a week to buy that almond butter at the grocery store. During the first three to five days of each month, work to keep your spending intact so that you have enough money budgeted for the entire month. Plan so that it's spread out based on what activities you have planned for the month. If you know you have a trip or big night out planned, you'll want to have that on your calendar so that it's allocated for. You don't want to find yourself eating eggs for dinner the last week of every month because you didn't budget for groceries the last week. I've been there a time or two and had to make it work with what we had. I will say that it's always disappointing when the last few days of the month approach and you didn't even leave enough money for one happy hour margarita. We would often plan dinner dates or "splurge" nights in advance to help keep us disciplined. This helped us avoid impromptu "hangry" trips to Chipotle or Chick-fil-A each week, thus saving money.

My 2 Cents #6
Cancel all those subscriptions that you don't actually need. Magazines, online subscriptions, courses, etc. All of the things that you're paying $9.95 for a month add up quick.

Yes, there will be times when you have to say no to going out with friends, but try and limit those occurrences by planning. To do this, I recommend setting aside $40 of your restaurant fund for spur of the moment gatherings. When you plan for these times you'll rarely have to say no; you'll have a plan and will be prepared. For the times that you can't make it work, don't worry. If you're like us, 98 percent of the people you know are also in debt and just aren't as committed to paying off their loans like you. Who knows, you might be the debt leader to set the example for the rest of your family and friends. Once people see your success and the fact that you're still living a life that allows you to enjoy yourself, they'll be knocking on your door looking for financial advice.

More Discipline, Less Debt

"We must all suffer from one of two pains: the pain of discipline or the pain of regret. The difference is discipline weighs ounces while regret weighs tons."

– Jim Rohn

Practicing discipline in spending is similar to practicing discipline in anything you do. Discipline is the act of training yourself for new behaviors. It has been said in <u>Psycho-Cybernetics</u> by Maxwell Maltz, that when starting a new fitness regime it can take as little as twenty-one days to make something a habit. Limiting your spending will take that same type of practice. You may find it challenging in the beginning because you don't want to give up the lifestyle that you're so used to. However, once you find that those items you've been spending money on are meaningless and your savings is growing, it makes it that much easier. It truly is adjusting your mindset and accepting a new way of living. Please remember that this new way of living is in no way bad or even difficult, it's only a *change* of living. More importantly, remember that this lifestyle change isn't permanent. This moment in your life will be a blink in time and when you come out of it your life will be that much more incredible.

A great way to change a habit is to visually compare the cost of things. For example: eating in versus dining out. I'll use an easy example and one that worked for us when we had to change our dining habits. If you look at buying a $10 bottle of wine at the store versus a $10 glass of wine at a restaurant, you're saving $20 on drinks alone by not going out. For dinner, you can buy a family platter of sushi at Wegmans for $23. The same meal would cost you upwards of $45 when dining out. You're still getting the enjoyment of the delicacies and the company.

If you're struggling and want to learn some quick techniques about habits and discipline, I highly recommend reading a book or two. After reading these books you'll find that many traits they discuss are already a part of you, they just haven't been uncovered yet. Some great books that helped us during this time are *The Power of Habit* by Charles Duhigg, *Willpower* by Roy F. Baumeister and John Tierney, *Your Best Year Ever* by Michael Hyatt, and *4 Disciplines of Execution* by Sean Covey, Chris McChesney, and Jim Huling.

My 2 Cents #7
Eat home as much as possible. You know when you go out and order a glass of wine and realize it's the same price as the full bottle you could've bought? The same is true for everything about your meal out. It's a luxury to eat out but American culture has turned it into our norm.

Paying It Off

The last day of each month is the day to make the big loan payment. I looked forward to this day all month, which may sound crazy. How could giving Sallie Mae $3,000 of our hard earned money be exciting? It's difficult to explain, but when you get in the groove and see the loans decreasing each month you'll find it exhilarating too. Starting out, it may feel more stressful than exciting when you are looking at $175,000 and watching it drop to

$170,000. Yes, it's still a very large number. However, never get discouraged when you see the amount that you have left to pay.

The next piece of advice I'm about to give, you absolutely must follow. After every milestone payment that is made, **you must celebrate**. It doesn't have to be a big celebration, but do something. Open a bottle of wine, "cheers" with ice cream, order take out. Do something. Having a reward will make this habit easier to create and something you actually look forward to.

For your bigger money milestones, you'll want to plan something bigger. I'm someone who likes to look forward to things to keep me motivated. Once you have paid off $25k, $50k, $100k, take a small weekend trip to celebrate your success. It allows you to feel like you're still enjoying your life AND becoming debt free. These weekends will also help test your ability to practice self-control when traveling and eating out (I'll get to the travel planning in more detail later).

My 2 Cents #8
Basic cable and internet will cost over $1,000 a year. I personally couldn't keep paying $160 a month for cable and internet. Do you watch $40 worth of TV each week? Probably not, especially if you're working and only home for a couple hours a day.

What is the Debt Snowball and Why Do Some Disagree?

You may or may not have heard of the debt snowball. The debt snowball is a technique used for paying off loans starting with the smallest loan to the largest regardless of interest rates. To do this you'll want to list all of your debt payments. For example:

Loan A: $500 (4.5% interest rate)
Loan B: $2,500 (7% interest rate)
Loan C: $10,000 (6.5% interest rate)
Loan D: $18,000 (6.5% interest rate)

Don't worry about interest rates when using the debt snowball method. The idea is to visualize the debt payments and start knocking them out one by one. If you have $550 to put towards loans at the end of the first month you can knock out Loan A completely and put the remaining $50 towards Loan B. Think of how you'll feel when you can completely cross a loan off of your debt list. It's pure motivation to be able to say that you've paid a loan in full. At the end of the following month, you find that you have $800 to apply towards loans. Your $2,450 Loan B can now drop to $1,650. In two more months' time you can wave goodbye to Loan B! In the beginning, I questioned the method because some of our interest rates for private loans were upwards of 9 percent. We ignored what we thought we knew about paying off loans with high interest rates. In our first few months, we started paying off those small loans. By doing so it showed us that the plan really did work. In reality, the difference in interest rates would only change the sum of the loan by a couple hundred to a thousand dollars. One by one we started crossing entire loans off the list. A large list of loans quickly became just a handful of loans. It looked a little something like this just a few months in.

~~Loan A: $1,800~~
~~Loan B: $2,200~~
~~Loan C: $2,400~~
~~Loan D: $4,800~~
~~Loan E: $5,200~~

Loan F: $8,900
Loan G: $22,000
Loan H: $36,500
Loan I: $48,000

If you start with your largest loan of $48,000 it could take you one to three years to see any movement on that loan. That isn't motivating. However, when you knock out eight loans before the $48,000 loan, you're feeling good and no one can stop you!

Psychology vs. Science

You might ask yourself why you would go against everything you've ever learned about interest rates? You might tell yourself that it doesn't make mathematical sense. Unfortunately, logic isn't what typically drives discipline. A "finance" friend of mine couldn't get past the fact that we would be paying off loans without considering interest rates. He couldn't get on board with the debt snowball because he was focused on numbers alone, not psychology. The gratification that we received when a full loan was paid off kept us hungry and disciplined. We found ourselves seeking ways to save and make more money to keep the snowball growing quicker. The psychological side has a lot more to do with getting this done than the logical side. This step of the process is critical. I encourage you to trust the system. Once you have seen it in action you will not be disappointed.

Eventually, once we were down to the last few loans, we did begin paying off loans with higher interest rates. At that point, there was just a small difference in the size of the loans and it didn't hurt us to pay off the smaller loans first. As long as you remain focused on the end goal the debt snowball will be a huge factor in your success and commitment to the debt-free journey.

CHAPTER 3:
FINDING WHAT'S IMPORTANT TO YOU

We all have different things that are important to us and what we're willing to spend the extra dollar or two on. This chapter includes short excerpts of my personal experiences and scenarios that we came across during our debt free journey. Some may be relatable and some may not. Know that this is my personal journey and your items of importance might be quite different. The point is that while you are on a budget, there's always flexibility based on your individual needs.

Traveling

As I mentioned earlier, traveling and experiences are what I look forward to most in life. I made sure to always budget accordingly so I could still take a vacation (or two) each year. For us, we budgeted $3,000 for travel for two people. Keep in mind that I work in hospitality so I get killer deals on hotel rooms which I completely take advantage of to make this lifestyle feasible. This allows us to budget a bit less because we often only need to buy the flight and budget very little on hotels. I still plan trips based on flight deals, location, and the miscellaneous spending that comes with a vacation. It's important to do the research when booking and look at what the hotels provide each day to make sure you choose the best deal. Do you receive complimentary breakfast? What is the daily parking rate? Are you located within walking distance of all attractions or do you need a rental car? These are all questions to ask yourself that could turn your inexpensive vacation into a budget breaker.

Personally, we don't plan for many tours or excursions when we travel. I like to get out and explore the city, but on my own time. My husband and I differ in this because he LOVES tours and wants to know all the history of a city. He loves a big bus tour and we have seen many cities on top of that big red bus (tickets are negotiable of course). We started doing morning runs when on vacation to get ourselves acclimated to the place we're in, rather than having to taxi around. The things you see while running around a city are so much greater! You see all of the local spots and the hidden gems that you otherwise wouldn't know were there. Many of us like to buy souvenirs and fall into the tourist attractions, feeling like we're missing something if we don't buy another coffee mug or keychain. In reality, those usually end up sitting on a closet shelf for the next three years until you stumble upon it during your spring cleaning. My advice is to save that money and use it where it counts.

I've found that the biggest expense while traveling is eating, which you can't avoid, nor should you try! I like to experience the local cuisine and enjoy my vacation and I do that by eating and exploring. If I'm being honest, I do pack snacks for the trip so I always have something in my bag. Protein bars, trail mix, and fruit are my go-tos. I've often gotten laughed at for this (including by my own husband who's the first to eat those protein bars!) but it saves on buying conveniences. It would be a shame to waste money by simply not being prepared. You'll soon discover that being proactive can lead to cost effective traveling. The things that I do are easy and don't actually require a huge lifestyle change. All that I do is make a plan to spend my money this way when I travel so that I get to enjoy every bit of the vacation. Do you notice the trend?

Plan + Budget = Fun.

Balling on a Budget

Like I mentioned earlier, traveling is the number one thing that I choose to spend my money on. By no means do I splurge when I travel, but I'm able to experience new places and enjoy myself while I'm there. Disclaimer: I am not staying at the Four Seasons Hotel or eating surf and turf every night. At all times, I have a lengthy list of places that I want to one day visit and from there I search out deals to travel to those places. There are so many tools at our fingertips that we can utilize to spend smart. My new favorite is a notification that I receive via email every single day. I should really unsubscribe because it has so many great deals that I want to snatch up! If you've heard of Scott's Cheap Flights then we are already on the same page. This website searches for the cheapest flights all throughout the world based on where your outbound destination is. Some days, it's an airline glitch and you only have one hour to buy the ticket and others are airlines running specials to fill seats. These are the times to take advantage of good deals and plan a trip.

Use it as a reward for getting to a payment milestone or a gift to yourself or significant other. For us, we claim that our trips are generally a "Christmas, birthday, and anniversary gift" all wrapped up into one since we don't buy gifts. We tend to get more enjoyment out of experiences versus the latest gadget. For years, I bought Michael gifts that ended up not being used and eventually we came to the realization that experiences were worth so much more. In fact, most of those gifts have recently been sold due to my new hobby of online selling.

Some other great sites I use are Hopper, Hotels Tonight, Cheap Caribbean, Gate1, and my personal favorite, Southwest's Low Fare

Calendar. Each of these platforms listed below are specific to the type of vacation you're looking for and have been life-changing for me.

Jeanna's Travel Deals

Hopper- This is an app that tracks flights and alerts you on the cheapest day to arrive and depart. It also lets you know when the flight price will begin increasing. You can choose a specific month and destination or you can leave it open to alert you to all destinations and dates. This is great if you have flexible travel dates or are open to experiencing any city that has a deal that day. I have witnessed round-trip flights for as low as $49. This is an app for the adventurous!

Scott's Cheap Flights- As I mentioned above, Scott's is a site that you subscribe to for free to receive updates on flight alerts that could save hundreds of dollars per ticket. These updates can be HUGE savings; potentially $500 or more depending on your destination. Be careful with this one and don't fall into the "$300 flight to Paris tomorrow?? I have to book it!" category. You might end up spending more by traveling constantly.

HotelTonight- This is an app that allows you to book last-minute hotels for the cheapest rates on the day of. This site gets the unsold hotel rooms that you can book while walking through the door. This is best used when you're in a city with no plans and are looking for a quick place to stay. All hotels are screened so you know that you're getting a great product for the best price.

Gate 1 Travel- If you're looking for a more extreme and lengthy vacation outside of the US for less, this is your site. Find travel packages that include airfare, transportation, accommodations, tours, and meals for a steal. Have you ever wanted to discover all of Thailand in ten days? And for $1,200? WITH AIRFARE? Yes, please! Sign me up. There's nothing more to say.

CheapCaribbean- This one is my jam! I'm a beach junkie and this website is a compilation of all of the Caribbean resorts; all-inclusive and with airfare. It compares the cheapest days and times to travel. If your dates are flexible you can save hundreds of dollars. If you don't have a destination in mind, this site also provides you with the rates for each location. There are a lot of options on this site and you can get sidetracked easily. The best thing to do when using this site is to have your budget set prior to searching. Tan away!

Apple Vacations- I have not yet used Apple Vacations myself, but know many friends who have had a great experience with it. Not only do they offer all-inclusive packages with flights, hotel, excursions, and transportation, but they will price match any offer that you find cheaper. Sounds like a win-win to me. I definitely plan on using it this coming year.

Groupon- Groupon is a site that offers so much more than travel deals. This is a place where you want to search for weekend getaways or short-term excursions. Typically, when I'm on Groupon I don't have a plan for what I want to do or where I want to go. Groupon helps make that decision for me. I search the parameters within a few hours of my location and in minutes I can have a vacation booked for half the price.

Southwest's Low Fare Calendar- This is the website that I use most frequently. It's best utilized if you have a destination in mind, but have some flexibility in your dates. You can choose the month that you're looking to travel and can see the most inexpensive dates to travel on the calendar. You might find that flying on a Thursday night saves you $200 versus flying out twelve hours later. If you have the ability to adjust your travel plans then this site will be golden.

My 2 Cents #9

Budget for all holidays. Christmas is hard; I get it. Be smart in your purchases and don't go crazy. Buy throughout the year when you find items on sale.

Giving

Gifts are our second largest periodic item and this doesn't include gift giving to each other. We both have large families and enjoy giving around the holidays. When you start to plan your periodic budget it'll surprise you just how many "present giving" occasions there are. It's important to us to give on holidays because it allows us to reciprocate all that our families do for us. Plus, we have cute nephews who we like to spoil! We don't go crazy with the gifts, but do spend an average of about $50 to $75 per person for each holiday. This includes Christmas, birthdays, Mother's and Father's Day, baptisms, baby showers, wedding showers, and the most expensive of all, weddings.

Depending on where you are in life, these occasions will ebb and flow. In 2017, we were heavily hit in the wedding gift budget area with so many friends getting married. In addition, I had countless baby and wedding showers to attend. Luckily, none of these events are ever a surprise. Each year, I have an idea of which weddings we'll be attending so that I'm able to plan for each. Again, do your homework and start planning. Count the number of weddings, showers, and holidays and come up with a number for your budget. If that number is $3,000 for the year, you'll be putting away $250 a month in your gifts periodic line item ($3,000/twelve months). For some, this category could be as little as $200 if you choose to opt out of gift giving for a few years, which is also a great option. Like I said, it depends on many individual factors like family size, what you celebrate, and where you are in life. If $200 is your annual gift budget, amazing!

Like Winston Churchill said, "We make a living by what we get, but we make a life by what we give." Over the course of our debt-free journey, we read several of Dave Ramsey's books to gain more knowledge and to stay motivated. On one of our many long car rides back to New York we were listening to Dave Ramsey's *The Legacy Journey*, which introduced us to tithing. At the time, Michael and I weren't avid churchgoers. Over the last year, God has become more influential in our lives. We started attending church more regularly after our wedding and even joined a "Small Group" that we attend once a week with other Christians our age. Reading *The Legacy Journey* reinforced the importance of tithing in our lives. On that day it became important to us to give back to the church. Listening to that book changed how we started living our lives and our financial plan. It gave us motivation as to what our lives could look like in ten, twenty, and thirty years. It gave us hope that by following a few simple steps we could live a very profitable life.

I truly believe there are only three things required to have a solid financial plan. Simply do the following: save, spend, and give. At the time, we weren't giving to anything or anyone, believing that every extra dollar must go towards loans. Growing up I didn't know about tithing, aside from the weekly collection at church. The tithe is giving 10 percent of your income to your church. Tithing is meant to be given free of a motive with nothing expected in return. If I'm being honest, that sounded like A LOT of money to be giving when we still had $100k to pay back to Sallie Mae. Who were we to be giving money when we were not debt-free ourselves? I know that this doesn't sound very Christian of me, but I was new to this and was still learning about financial planning.

By the conclusion of the book, we had discovered the many positives to tithing. We decided that it was important to us to give and to live a life that included tithing moving forward. We didn't initially commit to the 10 percent, but started giving 5 percent of our income to the church each month. We adjusted our spreadsheet, added a line item, and each month were able to give to our local church. It didn't feel like we were losing money or paying less to the monthly loans since it was included in our budget. The money was accounted for in the plan, the same as if it were being spent on clothing or groceries. I highly recommend reading a book on tithing and hearing some stories of those that feel strongly about it. It may change your perspective as it did ours. Remember, we were able to give 5 percent of our monthly income and still pay off $175,000. If that doesn't prove that this plan works and God looks out for you, then I don't know what does.

"Ditch the Dog": When You Have a Case to Defy the Rules

Do you have a cute four-legged furry friend? In our initial conversation with our finance coach, we talked about some of our larger expenses and where we thought we could cut back. During this conversation, we were told that we shouldn't have our just-adopted seven-month-old puppy. They thought it was a poor decision considering our large amount of debt and the costs that are associated with having a pet. Yes, all of that is true, but there was no way that I was finding a new home for my adorable little dog, Lola. We committed to making it work and even provided Lola with her own monthly budget. This would include her daily expenses of food, treats, and any additional dog necessities. In addition, her periodic budget was much larger, but that's the price you pay for love!

Within the annual "Lola budget" was grooming expenses, pet insurance, vet fees, and eventually boarding (doggy daycare). I am highly aware that she became even more expensive than planned, so keep that in mind if you're considering getting a dog. It's a hefty price we pay for puppy love. To save on grooming costs, we choose to get her groomed only twice a year, once in the spring and again in the fall. I'm 100 percent positive that she doesn't mind one bit! Pet insurance was an expense that served us very well and worked in our favor. Pet insurance is a personal decision, but I would take into consideration the following factors: the type of dog you have, their age, and your overall gut feeling since you know your dog more than anyone else. Our dog is an adopted basset-australian shepherd mix with high anxiety. She's the sole reason we had to move out of the city because she stopped drinking water to avoid having to go outside. We chose to go with pet insurance because we felt that she would be the type of dog who would need it. She would eat something and be sick. She was allergic to medicine the vet provided and had a bad reaction to it. Lastly, she tore her ACL in her knee and required surgery. Had we not had the pet insurance, we would have spent over $5,000 on surgery, medication, and appointments. Thank you, Pet Plan. On the flip side, my parents have had dogs for over twenty-five years issue free. I guess it's the luck of the draw!

My 2 Cents #10
Never buy bottled water; it's a waste of money and not good for the environment. I know this sounds like you're only saving $2, but think of when you're out and the bottle of water is now $5. Be prepared, always carry your own bottle with you.

Less Self Deprivation, More Happy Hours: Finding a Healthy Balance

It's important to find a healthy balance between self-deprivation and enjoying yourself when you go out with friends, co-workers, or family. If you start depriving yourself too much you might want to throw in the towel completely and give up on your debt. Throughout our debt repayment, I continuously had to keep myself in check by not going too extreme. I was so determined on paying off the loans that I would consume myself with every dollar that was being spent. Michael was better at finding a balance and helping me realize that I could go out and spend $20 at happy hour with my friends and not feel guilty doing so. It's important to know that while I was spending money having a glass of wine I wasn't splurging and still stayed within budget.

There are two sides of the spectrum: not depriving yourself (modestly) and going crazy and ordering that 42 ounce porter steak. Eating out was more challenging for me. I would look at the menu and even if something was $1 more than another item I would choose the more inexpensive item. If there was an option to add cheese or avocado to a burger 90 percent of the time I would say no. Looking back, did that $1 really make a difference? The answer is no. Self-deprivation doesn't win when paying off debt. We often had to tell ourselves that it's a marathon, not a sprint. I became a pro at finding the best deals in the city to fill my desire to enjoy a night out and would do so by spending less than $20. Wherever you live you'll find that most restaurants have daily deals during the week that can't be beaten. Find a local spot that does $5 burger night (my favorite), half off sushi before 7 p.m., or $2 tacos and $4 margaritas. Even now, after having paid off our loans, I still find it difficult to pay for an expensive meal when I know the deal I might be missing out on.

For thirty months, we committed to not ordering take out. For me, this wasn't too challenging because I was never keen on ordering delivery food. During my four years in college, I could count on one hand the number of times I ordered in. Not to mention that half of those times were ordering ice cream flurries. The things that can be delivered right to your college dorm! If I wanted to enjoy a meal from a restaurant, Michael and I physically had to go out and enjoy it. If I wanted to stay in at my house then I might as well save $25 and make dinner myself. Making the commitment to stop ordering take out could potentially save you $100 a month. When revamping our budget after the loans were paid, this was one category that we considered adjusting. Eating out and ordering take out is still what I would consider splurging so it still remains a small monthly amount. Remember, challenge yourself and commit!

My 2 Cents #11

Did you know a giant bag of carrots costs less than $3? Or that a bushel of bananas costs less than $1.50? Set a challenge and see what you can get your grocery bill down to for two weeks. It will be motivation!

CHAPTER 4:
TRIALS AND TRIBULATIONS.
I WILL SURVIVE.

"We buy things we don't need with money we don't have to impress people we don't like."

— *Dave Ramsey*

The Curse of Starbucks: The Coffee Conundrum

As I sit here writing at 6:30 a.m. with my freshly brewed Starbucks coffee that I made with whole beans and a french press, it's clear that I LOVE my coffee. And I LOVE Starbucks. Before making a budget you might think that buying a small coffee or latte a few times a week won't break the bank. You might be right, but it certainly won't help you pay off those loans any faster. These small changes that you're about to make will have a significant impact on the amount of cash flow that you have left at the end of each month. If you spend on average $12 to $15 on just coffee per week, you're looking at another $800 a year in savings. For us, it sounded like a habit that we could change so we committed to a very small "convenience" budget of $20 for the month. We started enjoying our weekend coffee mornings by using our french press and grinding the beans ourselves. We had a cappuccino machine given to us as a gift, as well as a slow drip coffee maker. You name it, we had it. It was time for us to make use of what we already had to save upwards of $1,500 on coffee between the two of us. For you, coffee purchases might not be relevant and you might think,

"Easy." Did we find ways to get our Starbucks coffee fix every now and then? Absolutely. When holidays came around and family asked what we wanted it was often the response of "Starbucks gift cards!"

Take a look at conveniences you buy and try and cut them out completely. In the last thirty months I rarely physically went into a convenience store or gas station. Those are the places that you walk in and walk out with $25 less in your pocket. The worst part is that you didn't even buy what you went in for. Get away from buying chips, soda, Gatorade, smoothies, etc. at a convenience store. The amount of money you'll save will be worth it.

My 2 Cents #12

Go on vacations that don't require a lot of spending. Enjoy and explore the natural scenery. Go to the beach where all you require is a house rental. All of your meals could be made in the house. What more do you need with the ocean right outside your door? Places that require a lot of spending once you get there are places like Disney and amusement parks. Avoid these places at all cost because once you get there you'll be spending twice as much as your cost to get there. Unless, it is your childhood dream of course!

My Friends Told Me I Had a Grandma Purse: Avoiding Temptation and Impulsive Decisions

Anywhere I go, even if it's to the grocery store, I'm prepared for hunger to hit me. You never want to be caught off guard! My purse will always contain one or more of the following: trail mix, an apple, protein bars or pretzels. You can determine where I'm going and for how long, by looking in my bag and seeing the number of snacks I have. Do I sound crazy yet? Possibly. However, I do this for two reasons.

1. 1. I always want to be prepared if I get hungry and want to have a healthy option to choose from.
2. I can get by on a protein bar instead of spending $10 at a fast food restaurant.

This is one of the tips that you might get ridiculed for. Embrace it! Soon enough your friends and family will be looking to you for that protein bar when you're out together and they didn't come prepared.

When going on trips, whether flying or driving, you should always go with a bag of goodies. Again, by being prepared you'll save money by avoiding those quick spending trips at rest stops. We often take long car trips because our family lives in Upstate New York and we live in Maryland. Nearly once a month we're driving five hours home and in the past thirty months we have stopped and eaten zero times. This is because I always have my go-to snacks. Depending on the time of day we're leaving I will always make us our meal for the road; egg sandwiches in the morning or salads for the evening. Not only are we saving money, upwards of $40 round trip, but our bodies are also appreciating us for not eating that Roy Rogers's burger and french fries.

Longer vacations require a bit more planning. On these, I still pack a substantial amount of food either in my packed luggage or purse. Michael has questioned the amount of food I can get through airport security in my purse. The airport is a whole world of temptation! Try and be strong and don't look left or right. That's a joke, but sometimes a reality if you feel that you don't have the discipline to get through the fifty eateries and stores as you walk to your terminal. Think of airport restaurants and gift shop prices. You know it's inflated because it can be. As people start their vacation they are feeling good and ready to spend money on anything that catches their eye. This includes that $8 magazine for the twenty minute read before getting on the plane and the $9 frozen yogurt that comes with cookie dough topping. This is a good place to practice your discipline and to be prepared. The real key is preparation. Have your meals and snacks ready to go. You should have already purchased your reading material or downloaded any of the million books circulating Amazon. You're in the zone. You got this.

Breakfast for Dinner? Yes, Please!
Eating Your Way Out Of Debt

Groceries and maintaining a healthy diet were one of our important buckets. We didn't plan on changing our diets significantly to save money, which meant we had to work harder to plan out our meals. There was no chance that hot dogs and frozen pizzas would be entering our lives. Nope, not having it. Each week, I would make a meal plan to include lunch and dinner meals. By doing this, I was able to shop for only the items I knew we would be using, which eliminated food waste. This also reduces excessive spending by wandering through aisles, looking at all of the things that you don't need. I would find ways to make meals that included a protein, but also went very heavy on vegetables that were in season.

If you have a garden then you're already one step ahead. When summer rolls around you will have a surplus of vegetables and will only need to shop for the basics. I was lucky enough to raid my dad's garden on trips home. Zucchini, eggplant, cucumbers, tomatoes, and squash were heavily consumed from June to September. When fall came around Michael was maxed out on zoodles and tomato salad (I highly recommend investing in a zoodle maker; they are truly life changing!). I know that we all don't have the luxury of having a garden in the backyard, but get creative and find ways of getting food outside of the four walls and fluorescent lights of the grocery store. There are so many "pick your own" vegetable farms out there. I guarantee that you can find one within twenty-five miles of your home. Take a day trip, pick your own spinach leaves, and stock up for the next three weeks! You'll find that by picking them fresh, the vegetables and fruit last much longer because the transportation window from the farm to the grocery store is eliminated. One of our new favorite finds is Hungry Harvest. This organization saves fruit and vegetables that aren't consider "show" worthy in stores and delivers them to your door step. No longer will dented tomatoes and miniature squash be thrown away!

Meal creativity is key so that you don't get bored with your meals. To stay on track and invested in the plan you have to make sure that it's still fitting with your lifestyle. If you're having trouble finding recipes there are so many blogs out there that specialize in eating on a budget. Check out Budget Bytes by Beth or The Frugal Foodie Mama by Carrie for some great ideas. I found that I really enjoyed cooking because I was going out of my comfort zone and eating meals that were more exotic and less repetitive. Another idea is to create a Pinterest board for the menus you'd like to try and update it weekly. See if you can try a new menu a week or host a potluck with friends.

Another trick when planning meals for the week is to make one giant meal of chili, stew, or soup. In the winter when it was cold, I started making a big meal to last the week. This not only saved money, but also time that could be spent on more important things each day. I would make turkey bean chili, lentil soup, vegetable soup, southwestern style chili, etc. I would see what was left in the refrigerator and throw it in a pot to make something delicious. With soup or chili, you can easily get six meals out of it, which is half of your week right there. I recommend actually making a list of what you have planned for the next seven days. List it out starting on Sunday with lunch and dinner meals so that you can visualize it. This helps you stay on track and leaves nothing up for question. It eliminates the last minute need to order out at night or spend $10 on a salad at work. This is an easy way to take the stress out of your week and to provide you with more valuable time.

My 2 Cents #13

Each week, take ten minutes to create your weekly meal plan. Plan out your lunch and dinner with the items you purchased for the week. This will keep your meals creative and allow you to be resourceful when cooking so that no items are wasted.

Like I mentioned, meal creativity and simplicity are key in our household. Let me start out by saying that I love breakfast. I would eat it for every meal if I could. Eggs, pancakes, yogurt, cereal, french toast, oatmeal. I don't discriminate. The great part about breakfast is that it's a very inexpensive meal to enjoy. On my weekly meal plan, I often require breakfast for dinner one night a week. This not only saves money, but a lot of time; especially when you get home and don't feel like pulling out your inner Emeril Lagasse. Throw together an omelet, add some yogurt, and you have dinner on a dollar! Groceries are one area that really requires a plan if you want to stay within budget each month. If you spend too much in the first week you'll be living off of rice and beans for the remainder of the month. I know that's not ideal, but it can easily be avoided with planning. Don't forget to shop around. Buy what's in season and look for stores that are having sales. Just remember that this is temporary and you'll only be making these sacrifices for a period of time, not your entire life. If you can make a few adjustments then I promise you'll succeed in your grocery budget and still have the ability to eat healthily. I live by the following: Less meat. More vegetables. Breakfast for dinner.

Making Due with What You Got: Minimizing Household "Needs"

"Love is... what I got. I said remember that."

— *Sublime*

This is an area where you can get creative and really cut your budget. Here, I like to take on the minimalist approach. Your household periodic budget can get extremely large if you start buying things like furniture and appliances. When in debt, those are the things that become wants, not needs. Does your couch provide comfort and your washer still wash clothes? If the answer is yes, then you have no need to buy new. Challenge yourself to keep the household budget at $500 per year. I promise that it can be done and I promise that it's actually simple. You may have just saved yourself $3,000 in one year by adjusting that single budget.

Speaking for someone who has moved several times and has been in this situation of needing furniture, I have a few great examples. In the six years that we've lived in Baltimore, we've moved to five different places. You might ask why, which is a great question. You might also think that it was a poor decision because moving costs money, sometimes an excessive amount of money. I would say that you're right about both, but each time we moved by ourselves and paid our friends in pizza and beer. We're now excellent packers and Michael even treats the physical part of the move like a CrossFit workout trying to make his best time. By doing this ourselves (and with family) we saved in moving costs, upwards of $1,000. Each of our moves ultimately came back to our budget and how much money we wanted to spend on rent. At one point we moved into a friend's home that was on the market to save some extra money and save them from a second mortgage. We stayed there until the house sold, which ended up being three months later. Hence another move to a more permanent environment, and again, for less money. It's obvious that moving is not an ideal situation, but if it's going to save money, then sometimes you have to bite the bullet and just do it.

Moving so often has forced us to be minimalists. In the past couple of years, we haven't bought any additional furniture knowing that it might not fit in the next place or it's just too difficult to move.

We've also steered away from buying extra furniture pieces because we think of the end goal of having to move it all again. We purchased a kitchen table on Craigslist and were given a used couch and coffee table from family. One of my living needs is to have an apartment that has a washer and dryer unit so that we don't have to spend a significant amount of money on large appliances. These are big expenses that we're waiting on until we have a home and the funds to purchase items that we want. If you're looking for larger household items there are so many options aside from buying new. Visit your local next-to-new shop, flea market, or go online. Go to an apartment complex on a Saturday when tenants are moving out. So many people are constantly moving and wanting to get rid of furniture that they will probably give it away for free. Just do your research!

My 2 Cents #14

Paint your own nails, do your own facials, let your hair be natural. This is an area of sacrifice for women, I know. I couldn't pay someone to do my nails when I could so easily do them myself. Of course, there are special times, which warrant the occasional treat. Yes, for my wedding, I did splurge and get my nails done. Otherwise, I went to the hair salon once a year (using a Groupon to find a great deal) and never did I get a facial. The one thing I wanted to do upon being debt free was book a spa day; massage and facial as a treat!

CHAPTER 5:
AS THE DEBT SNOWBALL ROLLED ON THE QUESTIONS ROLLED IN

Buying Used vs. Brand New: A Lesson in Assets and Liabilities

If you have a dad like myself who owns an auto shop and is a mechanic, it certainly has its benefits. However, I'm sure that 95 percent of you don't have this small luxury. Aside from the fact that he helped me out when getting an oil change or new tires, I also had some basic knowledge. From a young age, I knew the true value of a vehicle. I also knew that as soon as the car is driven off the dealer's lot its value depreciates. This means that the value that you paid for the car is severely diminished. You may have paid $20k for the car, but once it's bought, you're looking at a potential value of $17k or less. The point is that you may have just lost yourself $3,000. The bigger point that I'm trying to stress is that I wouldn't recommend buying a brand new car. A car is a liability in the fact that it depreciates every day. Some vehicles depreciate faster than others and you'll rarely hear someone say that they made a profit from selling a car.

The difference between assets and liabilities is that assets put money in your pocket while liabilities take them away. Think about how often you have to fix your car and put money INTO it to maintain it. You spend thousands of dollars on insurance, gas, and repairs every year. You won't be selling your car for more money than you purchased it to make a profit. Assets are things of value that will make you money. Assets don't depreciate, but often increase in profitability. Examples of assets are property and investments that get you a return on your money. In my personal experience, I have purchased five used cars and some that had as little as 13,000 miles on them. They are basically new. When shopping around for a car do your research. Is the need for the newest car only because you want to say that you bought a brand new car? Think about it. For example, compare a 2017 Honda Civic to a 2018 Honda Civic. Ask yourself if you can tell the difference. Unless the brand has completely remodeled the car it's likely that the cars look identical. You might have the argument of buying a car with zero miles on it. I would say that you could find a car one year older with 2,000 miles on it. That should not be a deal breaker. When looking at the cost of buying a brand new car for $20k or the one-year-old car for $14k that looks identical, it's a no brainer. Be smart in all of your purchases from the type of milk you buy to the type of car you buy.

My 2 Cents #15

Learn to change your own oil and do small repairs. Replace your windshield wipers. Be your own car wash. These small tasks will save you a significant amount of money in the long run. Every dollar saved helps!

Buying vs. Leasing: Finding What Works For You

During our thirty months of paying off our debt, we ended up having to purchase three different vehicles due to a few unexpected life events. We moved outside of the city and Michael started his full-time job, which required us to both have cars to drive to work.

Prior to this, we had lived within walking distance to his university and my job so our car was rarely used. Michael's father let him use a 98 Honda Civic that he had just bought. The car was valued at no more than $1,000 dollars. It wasn't pretty, but allowed him to drive nearly 60 miles a day. Eventually, the car died with his brake pads literally falling off at one point. I didn't have to worry about him getting too much attention from other women on his rides to and from work. This wasn't ideal, but allowed us to put more money toward loans during that period of time. Shortly after, Michael bought a used car, a 2008 Fusion, from his grandfather's auto shop for $5,500. This was an unforeseen expense in the spring of 2017, but we had no other option as we both needed reliable vehicles to travel to work. This is a great example of how our emergency fund served its purpose.

At this point, Michael was traveling to Virginia for work every day, putting 115 miles on his car, per day. The increase in mileage was due to a new job offer that he could not resist. In the midst of this Michael also got into a bad car accident with my car totaling it the weekend before our wedding day. This led to another car purchase. As a result of all of these car mishaps, we went back and forth several times on whether it was smarter to lease or buy a vehicle. Those that lease vehicles strongly believe that it is the better option, but on the flip side, those that always buy feel that their way is better. In our experience and where we are in our lives buying a car was the better option because you own the product versus renting it. Would you rent a house if you could afford to buy? Oftentimes, people lease a vehicle because they want a really expensive car that they can't actually afford to buy. If they had the money to purchase it I'm 99 percent sure that they wouldn't have a lease. Leasing could be a good option if you rarely drive and don't have a high mileage during your lease. If you're debt free and want to drive a really nice car for a year that's another great time to lease. Hey, if a Mercedes is that one thing that makes you enjoy life to the max then, by all means, make that your biggest budget item and cut somewhere else.

There are many resources that can provide you with information to help make the right choice for you. The Balance is a site that provides some great material and can answer some of the questions you might have. Some of the pros and cons from the site are listed below:

Buying Pros	Buying Cons
You own the car and can do what you choose	Higher monthly payments* UNLESS paid in full
Drive as many miles as you want	Unexpected maintenance costs
Potential to trade in or re-sell for a greater value	Responsible for selling or trading in the car
Can drive the car for years to make it worth your while	You have the same car for years

Leasing Pros	Leasing Cons
You get to drive a new car every two years	You can only drive a set number of miles
You are protected by warranty	**You will pay more in the end with your payments**
You don't have to worry about selling the car	You must properly maintain your car
Monthly payments could be lower	You must have a stable source of income

https://www.thebalance.com/pros-and-cons-of-leasing-vs-buying-a-car-527145

My 2 Cents #16

Buy your household items in bulk or through a wholesaler. This includes dish soap, hand soap, paper towels, laundry detergent, toilet paper, and tissues. If you want to take it a step further stop buying non-essential paper goods altogether. Save by using real dishes and real hand towels.

How 'Bout that Side Hustle? How Everyone Can Be Their Own Entrepreneur

Now more than ever we have the ability to become entrepreneurs and make money from the comforts of our own home. The internet, specifically blogging, has opened up a new world of money just waiting to be made. Instead of just finding ways to save money, take a look and see what ways you can **make** more money. We're living in an era that allows us to make additional income through the click of a mouse. Consider the extra time that you have available each week and determine how you could increase your income. Weigh the amount of time and effort you want to spend against the return on investment. You might have time for a second job in the evenings. This will require a commitment and take up a large amount of your time. However, the pay will be steady and there is no risk regarding how much your income will increase; it's typically a set number. You could work overtime at your current job to increase your overall salary. You could sell items from your home that you no longer need on Poshmark, Etsy, eBay, Letgo, OfferUp, or Craigslist. You could start your own business or write a blog and work towards paid advertisements. You could sell LuLaRoe, doTerra, Arbonne, Mary Kay, Rodan + Fields, or Scentsy. You could babysit, nanny, or walk dogs part time. You can even take online surveys! The list goes on.

The amount of free time that you have will determine what type of side hustle you can make work in your life. If you've ever listened to millionaire entrepreneur Gary Vaynerchuk then you know that we have eighteen hours in a day to make money. Even if you have a full-time job or are a mom with two kids and have to make dinner, run to soccer practice, and put the kids to bed; that still leaves you with a little bit of extra time to hustle and make extra money. You might not have as much time as someone with a lesser mental load, but use those three hours you have an evening productively. I didn't start putting this into practice until the end of our debt-free journey. I know that I missed out on making thousands of dollars. I can only give you detailed insight into what I have actually done myself which was selling old items to make extra cash.

Selling Old Items: An easy and time efficient way to make money is to sell things. Take one hour or take as little as ten minutes out of your day and start selling things. We are living in an era that literally puts the rest of the world at our fingertips. You can sell items on eBay, Amazon, Craigslist, Facebook, and Facebook Online Marketplaces. There are so many channels out there to utilize and there are so many people looking to buy. I started this myself by cleaning out my closet of items that I knew were valuable and that I hadn't used in at least a year. Why does a person need multiple iPads, cameras, cell phones, and gaming systems? The answer is simple. WE DON'T. I found my very first iPad from 2009 buried deep in my closet under countless gadgets, old cell phones, and chargers. I quickly found that the "first generation" iPad is worth $140. Sold. I gathered all of my old cell phones from the last ten years and sold those online through Gazelle. Phones that had completely shattered screens which otherwise would have been thrown in the garbage still made me $35. I sold an unused espresso machine, iPad keyboard, DVDs, camera accessories, and skis. Not only was I able to make some extra money, but I felt better getting rid of the things that were being unused and selling them to others to enjoy.

My 2 Cents #17
**Sell old items in your house that are taking
up wasted space. Game changer.**

Cashing in Those Credit Card Points:
Choosing Paper or Plastic

The common dilemma of using credit cards versus cash. This is a hot topic that can be fought tooth and nail, but will ultimately be decided by you as an individual. I am pro-credit cards if used responsibly. How do I define responsible? Paying off the full balance within two weeks of a purchase, having a card that doesn't require an annual fee, and never incurring any interest charges. Lastly, only have one. I choose to use a credit card solely for the reward points that can be earned for cash back on travel. If you feel that you don't want to worry about paying another bill, I would avoid credit cards completely. As soon as I make a purchase I am quick to pay it off immediately so that I am not charged any interest fees. With that being said, it takes a lot of spending ($7,500) to earn ($100) back. Let's face it, credit card companies are not stupid; they know what they're doing and will rarely be outsmarted by the consumer.

Aside from using credit cards for the value they return, it has less of an emotional impact when you swipe a piece of plastic versus paying in cash out of your pocket. Thus bringing us back to psychology versus science. Cash is not actually more valuable than a credit card—it's all money—but how your brain interprets spending will have a significant impact on your success. In my personal experience, using cash quickly changed my spending habits. Think of the last time you went shopping and paid with cash. Did you feel it a little bit more than paying with a card? Did you question whether you really needed to buy that coat when you found you only had $10 left in your pocket? We found that by using cash for purchases it was harder to spend the money. Harder to spend money?? Yes, I said it. Make yourself pay with cash if you want to save money because it will make every purchase harder which is what we want. If you want to take it a step further you can use the envelope system, where you have physical envelopes designated for each purchase (clothing, restaurants, groceries, gas, etc.). Each time you make a purchase take out the envelope and remove the cash. I guarantee you'll save so much more if you follow this step and commit to paying with cash only.

My 2 Cents #18

**Avoid shopping. If you don't have self-control just don't go.
I followed this practice often. I used to like to wander into
stores on the weekend, but now I just don't go unless I have
a purpose for going.**

The Time We Almost Bought a House

If you aren't a homeowner you have likely considered buying a house at least five times a year. I know we have. About a year into our loan repayment plan we were feeling confident and thinking that a house might be a great investment. We thought that we would save money by paying a mortgage instead of renting. We were thinking that it would be a good long-term investment. We knew what Dave Ramsey said about buying a house when still in debt, but it sounded so enticing. I was envisioning granite counter-tops, repainting walls, and learning how to put up a kitchen backsplash. We started popping into open houses and "liking" houses on Zillow. It was all a beautiful dream. Eventually, we got a reality check and realized that we were still at least $70k in debt. We didn't have money for a down payment, we didn't have money for closing costs, and we definitely didn't have the time or money to fix up any part of a house. Yes, there are many positives to owning a home like having a mortgage that is half of your rent or investing in something that can provide you with a great return later in life. However, when you don't have enough money to pay off your debt, you don't have enough money to own a home. In reality, your home really isn't an asset. It is a liability. It does not generate an income and you likely won't make any money on it unless you bought it for an absolute steal.

Looking back on that "home buying reality check" I realize that we were getting ahead of ourselves. We had good intentions to save money long term, but we were jumping ahead in Dave's "baby steps" for getting out of debt. We knew all of the golden rules from following Dave Ramsey's program (which you can find below) but lost sight of our goal for a brief moment in time. If this happens to you, talk it through, weigh the pros and cons, and eventually come back down to earth. We all need a reality check once in a while.

Rules on When to Buy a House:

1. You're debt free
2. You have three to six months of expenses in your emergency fund
3. You have cash for a 10 to 20 percent down payment on a fifteen-year fixed mortgage
4. You're paying cash up front, or your mortgage payment is no more than 25% of your monthly take-home pay. https://www.daveramsey.com/blog/buy-vs-rent-myths-busted

My 2 Cents #19
**Buy generic. Generic food, generic soap,
generic hair supplies. They're all the same.**

What Are You Waiting For?

Michael and I dated for over eight years before we got engaged. After he finished school we were buried in debt. We made the decision to wait and get married when we were debt free. This would allow us to have a big wedding with family and friends, enjoy the wedding planning process, and have an amazing honeymoon! Fast forward to now where we have already celebrated our one-year anniversary. This means that we did not follow this plan. This is one decision that Michael made on his own and I am so glad that he did. It's true what they say about timing never being perfect and to just go for it.

We started the road to being debt free prior to getting engaged. We had our spreadsheets and budget in line. We were even planning for a wedding years down the road in our periodic budget. I thought it was realistic and logical to pay off our debt before getting married and spending even more money. However, plans don't always work the way you imagine and sometimes it's for the best. One day while Michael was talking to his uncle on the phone his uncle asked the question, "What are you waiting for?" When Michael thought about it his only answer came back to money which didn't seem like a very good response. After that conversation, he made plans to buy a ring with money he had in savings and the rest is history. You can imagine my shock when he actually did propose because it clearly was NOT in the plan, but we made it work.

To be honest, we made it more than work. We were able to have an amazing wedding with all of our family and friends back home in New York. We were extremely lucky to have our parents pay a substantial portion of the wedding, but also put down about $20,000 of our own. We had a year to save. We revamped our spreadsheet to increase our wedding budget to save more monthly. I kept track of every dollar spent and created a separate wedding budget so that I knew where our money was going. Rather than renting a lot of the usual wedding décor and necessities we found that buying them was more cost-effective. My dad, being the creative craftsman he is, was able to recreate every Pinterest item that I found. We bought linen online for less than half the rental price and it's the purchase that keeps on giving (to other friends getting married). A family friend offered to purchase our flowers from a wholesaler and created beautiful centerpieces right in the hotel the day before. There were ways we could have saved on food, but that was one area that I wanted to leave alone. You could do food trucks, BBQs, stations, etc. and those are great, unique, money-saving options for a wedding. Sit down with your fiancé and parents to determine a budget and from there decide on the top three things that are important to you on your wedding day.

From that moment on you'll know where you are open to making sacrifices and can start planning for your dream wedding. Pinterest, Wedding Recycle, and Tradesy are all great sites to get your creative juices flowing!

My 2 Cents #20

Stop buying all of the "need it now" gimmicks. Have you heard of the Apple Watch, the Instapot, the Fitbit, and iPhone X? Of course you have. Don't feel like you need to buy these very expensive items that everyone is raving about. They're not important.

To Invest or Not to Invest?

One of the big questions that we faced was regarding investing our money while we were still in debt. This is one area that isn't simply black and white. If you're following the Dave Ramsey program he will tell you to pay off your debt before putting money towards a 401k or any type of retirement plan. We veered from this plan just slightly because some opportunities are too good to pass on. The company that I work for matches up to 3 percent of what I put into my 401k. If I put in $10 from my paycheck they put in $10. In this scenario, I would be making what I like to call "free money." I was not willing to eliminate my 401k and lose out on a company match. Michael, on the other hand, didn't set up a 401k with his company because there was no added benefit to doing so. We looked at the money that would be coming out of his paycheck and into retirement and it didn't make sense for us. Everyone has different benefits from their company, so you can make those choices based on what fits your needs and what the long-term benefit will be. Seeking assistance from a financial advisor or your HR department is well worth the time.

My 2 Cents #21
Stop paying for cable and internet and save over $2,000 a year. Can you cut it out completely? It's easier than you might think and you'll find that you have so much more time.

CHAPTER 6:
PLANNING FOR THE UNFORESEEN: KNOWING WHEN NOT TO BE FRUGAL

Learning Car Insurance the Hard Way

When we first moved to Baltimore we shared one car because we lived downtown and traveled less than a mile to work and class. I had car insurance that allowed me to have the cheapest premium I could find. I was naïve and confident that we wouldn't be getting into any accidents and that my dad could fix any other problems that might arise (even living five hours away). I tell you this story so you can learn from my mistakes. Invest in good insurance and always have an emergency fund.

One morning that we had a trip home planned, I walked outside and couldn't locate our car. I called Michael upset asking where he left the car because it wasn't on the street where it was supposed to be. I looked up and down the streets of Baltimore growing frustrated and then becoming more anxious by the second. After coming to the realization that the car was gone, I called the tow company to check and see if it was towed. Sure enough, they had my car after it was reported stolen and left on a street still running with no one in sight. At the time, I didn't have comprehensive coverage on my car insurance, not expecting to have my car stolen. This was a very expensive lesson to learn after retrieving the car, paying $250 for the tow and another $1,000 for a new starter that was ripped out when it was being stolen. These are the situations that you don't expect to happen until they do. Luckily, we had money in our emergency fund so we could get the car fixed right away. Had we not had that money we wouldn't have been taking the car home and would have had bigger struggles ahead.

Insurance is now something that we spend a greater deal of money on because we aren't in a place to pay for something that could potentially be so much greater than $1,000. One of the first steps when starting the Dave Ramsey plan is to look at each of these expenses. Every single item that you pay for should be the best bang for your buck. You'll find that you might be paying a higher premium at an insurance company for their brand versus a local insurance company that provides greater coverage for the same price. Take a day to do your research and compare plans. For assistance and to see the difference in types of coverage try https://www.daveramsey.com/elp/auto-insurance to find what's best for you.

My 2 Cents #22
Reevaluate your health and car insurance. Is it the best deal that you can get for where you are? Many of the big brand companies cost a premium just for the name. I completely changed my insurance carrier when I found that I was paying the same price and not getting nearly the same amount of coverage as others.

Medical Insurance

At the age of twenty-six, when I was sadly released from my parents' health insurance, I had a world of learning to do. I never chose my own insurance plan before and didn't know the difference between an HMO, a PPO, an HSA, or an FSA. Now I'm just throwing out acronyms, but you get the idea. There was A LOT to learn. Much like car insurance I also didn't understand what the high deductibles were and what I would be paying in co-pays. Hell, I didn't even have a primary doctor and hadn't had one for the past five years. I was quick to look for the cheapest plan I could find, check the box on the computer, and be done. While it may have saved me a few dollars a month I was setting myself up for a potential money crisis.

I wasn't at the point in my life where I had an emergency fund of $10,000 if something were to actually happen to me. I was under the impression that as a young and healthy adult I had nothing to lose and the cheapest insurance plan would be best. After some further research and talking to several people I found the opposite to be true. If something were to happen and you don't have the funds needed you could put yourself in so much more debt in the blink of an eye. One car accident and an ambulance ride to the hospital can hit you with a $40,000 bill. Often times we use the "that will never happen to me" excuse. Until it happens. These are the situations to avoid if you want to be smart with your finances. The way to win is by minimizing your losses. One wrong decision in the world of medical insurance can be life-changing. It can be extremely difficult to bounce back from a loss that large when you're trying to build your savings account and pay off debt. Spend the extra $50 a month and I promise it will pay off in the end.

Initially, we weren't paying the extra $50 a month and we experienced the negatives that come with NOT minimizing our losses. Michael had an unexpected allergic reaction that required a hospital visit and a few $800 epi pens. The hospital bills could have been so much worse, but luckily at that point, we both had jobs that provided us with a comfortable insurance policy. From that point on, we chose the more expensive insurance plans that cost roughly $1,000 more a year. It's true that you might be 100 percent ok for one year never needing to visit the doctor—that is something to be proud of. However, don't assume the next year will be the same and adjust your insurance just because of that. Unless you're willing to potentially pay thousands of dollars out of pocket and have the emergency fund to do so, keep yourself safe. Pay the extra few dollars a paycheck to feel comfortable.

You read earlier that I have a dog named Lola who is the light of my life. I grew up with dogs all my life, but never knew about pet insurance and the benefits of it. As an adult and now fully responsible for my own pet I had to do some research and weigh the pros and cons of purchasing pet insurance. I spoke to several people that had pet insurance and also those that didn't, all with very strong opinions. Pet insurance is great as it covers emergencies, surgeries, rehab, stitches, and more. However, it doesn't cover any of the usual services that a pet requires when going to a vet, like shots and annual checkups. When deciding what to do it came down to the same question that I asked myself when choosing our medical insurance. Could I afford to pay for a life-threatening emergency for my dog out of pocket? Was I willing to pay $10,000 for a surgery that could save my dog's life if needed? It's tough to say, but the question comes down to putting a price on your animal's life. I wasn't ok with the fact that I might one day have to make that decision. I wasn't going to put myself in a situation where I would have to choose Lola or a $10,000 vet bill.

I signed up for pet insurance, agreed to the $420 annual premium and couldn't be happier that I did. The $35 a month gave me peace of mind that I would never be in a position that I couldn't afford proper care. The pet insurance actually paid for itself when Lola had to have knee surgery to repair a torn ACL. A $5,000 surgery was easily covered and I didn't have to question if she would be limping for the rest of her little puppy life.

There are many types of insurances out there that are less popular, but equally as useful. We all know about car insurance and medical insurance because we're required to have them. Some other common examples of insurances that you might be less familiar with are companies that deal with roadside assistance, renters insurance, identity theft, travel insurance, phone insurance, and warranties on products. These are just a few that you might want to research a bit more to keep yourself out of any unforeseen large expenses in the future.

My 2 Cents #23
Don't use convenience stores. Never. Not even for a candy bar or a soda. Just by walking into the store you'll be persuaded to buy items you don't need.

CHAPTER 7:
I'M DEBT FREE! NOW WHAT?

You did it! In the last few months leading up to our debt-free scream, we were doing everything we could to make additional money. This is when I really started digging through our items to see what might be of value to sell online. When the end is in sight you'll feel the most motivated to pay off as much as you can. If you're like us you'll want every extra dollar to go towards your loan payments. You might decide that the extra glass of wine or Chipotle bowl isn't worth it this month. You might want to pass on your haircut or become a vegetarian for the month to save on groceries. I might sound crazy, but when you get to this point in your debt-free journey call me up and tell me how you feel. Picture your last loan payment sitting at $4,800. Once that's paid off you will be debt free. Your life will be changed and open to new possibilities. You might start imagining all of the extra cash flow you'll have per month now that you don't have to put it towards loans. It might be $1,000 or it could be $4,000 more going into your savings PER MONTH. Enjoy the feeling and the excitement or even celebrate by doing something big! Just remember that now is not the time to throw away everything that you've learned about your finances.

My 2 Cents #24
Use Groupon! Like I said, I always used this app to find hair salons, activities, and even products at Christmas time. Don't get sucked into buying things on here you don't need; stay focused.

401k, IRA, Roth IRA, Mutual Funds?

You'll recall from Chapter 2 the steps listed from Dave Ramsey's debt-free living. After conquering Steps 1 through 3, you're ready to take on Step 4: investing. Don't be worried when you get to this step. This is a huge accomplishment and you should be proud!

Step 1: $1,000 cash in a beginner emergency fund
Step 2: Use the debt snowball to pay off all your debt, but the house
Step 3: A fully funded emergency fund of three to six months of expenses
Step 4: Invest 15 percent of your household income into retirement
Step 5: Start saving for college
Step 6: Pay off your home early
Step 7: Build wealth and give generously

You might wonder why all of the retirement plans have acronyms and why there are so many. Please know that it's not to make our lives more difficult, but to offer options based on where we each are financially in our lives. This site, thebalance.com, provided me with a broad understanding of the different retirement options.

Upon getting my first job and sitting with Human Resources I knew that a 401k was like a savings account for retirement. At twenty-three years old there was little else I knew aside from the fact that 3 to 5 percent of my paycheck would be going into my 401k instead of my bank account. What that would produce I never actually knew. When I looked at my statement a year later I was pleasantly surprised to see how much money I had accumulated in my 401k. If you work for a company that matches your contribution, then I highly recommend putting in the maximum amount for the match. That is one of the huge benefits that employers offer and you don't want to miss out on that money.

After your loans are paid off you'll want to dive into your finances in greater detail. Before you were trying to get out from underneath your debt, but now you're starting with a clean slate and have the opportunity to make the best financial decisions moving forward. The worst thing you can do is let all of your hard work go to waste by not being proactive for your future. Set a goal of how much money you want to have saved when you retire and work backward to determine how you'll get there. Once you have a goal then you can start working on a plan. I highly recommend meeting with a financial advisor at this point to help lead you in the right direction and figure out the best options for you. I'll briefly highlight each of the retirement plan options so that you have an idea of what might be your best fit. If needed, you can find in-depth detail on thebalance.com.

IRA (Individual Retirement Accounts) - This is an investment account that allows your money to be used for investing in stocks, mutual funds, etc. However, you'll pay a large amount of income taxes on the withdrawn money at retirement.

Roth IRA - The best thing about this account is that it offers tax-free growth and any income made doesn't need to be reported. These contributions are made after tax but you have the option to withdraw money at any moment without any penalties or fees. Max contribution per year is $5,500.

*Now that you have some extra cash, this is a great place to invest because it'll provide a great tax break.

401(k) - This plan is likely the one that you're currently contributing to or have heard of in the workplace. This allows you to contribute a portion of your pre-taxed paycheck to a retirement savings plan. This lowers the amount of income that your taxes are based on. However, if you withdraw money from this plan prior to retirement it could be heavily taxed taking away a large portion of what you have earned. Max contribution per year is $18,500.

Roth 401(k) - A Roth 401(k) combines features of the two and has only been around for a few years. This account has the contributions come from your after-tax paycheck instead of your pre-tax salary. An important note here is that Roth 401k contributions have no limit, unlike a Roth IRA.

But I Don't Even Know What a Stock Is...

Don't worry, neither did I. This is where you start using your resources and reaching out to those who have spent years studying finance. Now that you have extra money coming in you want to be smart with where it goes. What's the point of having money sit in a savings account when it can be sitting somewhere else doubling or tripling itself? I don't know enough about the stock market or investing to write anything of real value. What I can tell you is that I know the importance of investing and growing your funds.

While you can buy stock on your own, I would make sure that the appropriate amount of funds are being placed in your Roth IRA ($5,500) and 401k first. From there, consult with a financial advisor to determine whether or not investing in the stock market is right for you. Seeking the advice of a fiduciary is highly recommended. Fiduciaries are required to make decisions that are solely in your best interest. Often times a conflict of interest may arise when working with a broker. Many brokers receive a commission when investing your money in certain stocks.

Investing and putting your money into places that produce more money will be the difference between being "comfortable" and "rich" when you retire. If you want to live a fabulous life, travel, have a second home on the beach, and give to those who are less fortunate than you are, then don't discount this final step in your financial journey. Some might say that this is the biggest and most influential step. Now that you're officially debt free you have the ability to change your life and make choices that aren't solely centered on every dollar. You might have some room to allow for greater risks, which we know, could bring greater returns. Michael always tells me "scared money don't make money." Obviously, there is a balance to everything that we do in life, especially with spending. However, depending on how you envision your future this final investing step could be the game changer for your next thirty years.

Almost a month after we became debt free we set up an appointment with a financial advisor to go through our investment options and to help us with our taxes. I had always used the quick and easy option of TurboTax. This time, we wanted to see what benefits there were to meeting with an actual living human versus a computer. I will say that planning for retirement requires in-depth research. You want to be aware of where your money is going and how you want your life to look when you turn fifty-nine (or maybe you envision retiring at forty-five). Whatever the age is that you hope to retire, make sure you're putting enough money away and doing so in the smartest way possible. Eventually, you could end up living off of your investments and growing your income by not having to physically work another day in your life. If that doesn't make you want to call up a financial advisor in the next hour I don't know what will.

CHAPTER 8:
RE-ADJUSTING OUR BUDGET
AND OUR MINDSET

So You Want to Buy a Mercedes

Once you become debt free I like to say that the world is your oyster! As long as you maintain some aspect of a plan. If you thought you were done with budgets now that you are debt free you're very wrong. Sorry. You may decide that now is the time to put all of your hard-earned money towards something you've been wanting for years. You've settled on driving around a 2003 Chevy Impala with 150,000 miles on it for the last seven years. It got you through thousands of commutes, long trips to summer vacations, and did all that you could have hoped for. But it wasn't always the coolest and hottest car in the lot. You can now start to plan for that Mercedes or Mustang that you've been dreaming about for years. I'm not a car person by any means, it's just not my thing. I say this because I don't know what the actual cost of a (semi-used) luxury car is. If you estimate $50,000, start planning to save at least 50 percent for a down payment over the next year and soon enough you'll be able to buy that car and have it paid off in just two years' time. Remember, don't veer too far from what you have learned. Ideally, you would want to pay fully in cash or have such a large down payment that the interest rate is nearly nothing. From there, you'll want to immediately start paying the balance so that it's paid off as fast as possible to avoid racking up any interest and additional debt. As long as you plan out these larger purchases you'll not only be able to buy things you only dreamed of, but buy them responsibly.

My 2 Cents #25
Get outside and do activities. Hiking, running, yoga. These are all free and you can do them right outside your door.

Is There Room for Organic Chicken?

Now that you have a fresh start and your Excel sheet has all zeros, you'll want to adjust your budget to give yourself more of your wants that you've let go of over the past few years. The first thing that we did after our weekend celebration of being debt free was reconfigure our monthly budget. We looked at the areas that we felt could use a larger budget and adjusted. Right away I knew the two categories that I wanted to increase were groceries and restaurants. Every month those were the two categories that we struggled to stay within budget. We took our restaurant budget from $200 to $300 per month and our grocery budget from $290 to $330 and added in a separate category for protein bars and supplements (which used to fall under groceries). This small increase allowed us more freedom to buy what we wanted, but still kept us focused on tracking our money spent so that we didn't go crazy.

Every grocery shopping trip that Michael and I took together would result in the same silly argument about buying the expensive organic chicken at $4.49lb versus the nonorganic chicken at $1.99lb. Not only did this make me want to go to the grocery store on my own, but bringing him along would lend itself to a larger receipt at checkout. The first time we went grocery shopping after becoming debt free, we once again approached the meat section and had the option of organic versus nonorganic chicken. I'm not going to lie, I still put up a fight on which chicken to buy. In the end, he won and we walked out the door with the $15 pack of chicken rather than the $9 chicken. He told me that our bodies would be thanking us later. I tell you this story because throughout our journey Michael let me buy the cheaper chicken because we were set on spending as little as possible. We had a budget to maintain and $15 chicken wasn't going to get us there. However, when we finally reached our goal and had a few extra dollars to put towards groceries the organic chicken was a done deal.

I am still extremely conscious of what I choose to buy and make sure to stay within our new budget. Picture yourself not having a budget and not having to track your spending. You would have no one and nothing holding you accountable for the money coming out of your account. When this happens you'll quickly find yourself spending more than you make and working yourself back into debt. Once you come out of debt you have to commit to never going back there. Ever.

The Ability to Give Selflessly

Giving was a part of our budget where we contributed the bare minimum of what we felt we could do. One of the greatest feelings after paying off our budget was that we could now give more. We could give to people, donate to charity, and buy more for family and friends. Tithing was still important and now we had extra money to give to people and organizations that were meaningful to us. If a situation came up where we wanted to give, we no longer had to question how it would affect our monthly payments. This was a great feeling. We were able to change our mindset and re-adjust our budget so that charity became a periodic budget rather than just one monthly payment. It gave us the flexibility to give $100 here and $200 there whenever a situation arose. Prior to completing our debt-free journey I never would have considered giving on a monthly and yearly basis. I wouldn't have been giving to the church or setting aside money to give to charities and those in need. Not only did I learn key factors in how to manage money, but I learned so many greater life lessons about how to be less selfish when it came to money. Half of the fun in making money is being able to use it. We quickly learned that we didn't need a substantial amount of money to live our lives and that as long as we had what we needed, we could give to those in need as well.

This quote is one of my favorites and one that I feel couldn't be truer. "*We buy things we don't need with money we don't have to impress people we don't like*" (Dave Ramsey). If you're one of the few people that can say this doesn't apply to you, mazel tov! As human beings, we actually need very little to live. Not just survive, but live. This always brings me back to other countries outside of the United States and I think of how much we have when compared to many. Those in less developed countries are still living and likely living on just a few dollars a week. If we can't figure out how to live off of thousands a week something must not be right. I say this to reiterate the fact that you and I don't need to just keep spending our money to impress other people. Yes, we all work hard and should reward ourselves for the time we spend. However, when you take a look at your next few purchases I think you will also find that you might want to do without and put your money towards a meaningful act.

My 2 Cents #26
**Eat less meat. Live off of vegetables for a month and
you'll notice your grocery bill will be chopped in half.**

Lastly, Enjoy Life

In the end, what I've learned most is that money shouldn't be the
end all be all. We shouldn't live our lives constantly worrying
about what we have or what we don't have. We shouldn't be
staying up at night thinking about how to make more money or
how bills are going to get paid. As long as there's a plan you won't
have to worry one more day about money. Plain and simple. Enjoy
what you have and do what makes you happy. Plan out what is
important to you and what you want to get out of your life so that
you don't feel like you are ever restricted.

The goal of this book is to give you hope that you can get out of
debt quickly if you commit and make a plan. However, the greater
and more important goal of this book is to show you that you
don't have to diminish your quality of life to make it happen. I
wanted to share my experiences, both the good and the bad, to
help shed light on how simple it is to save money and live on a
budget. Yes, you'll face challenges, but within the first few months
you'll learn how to adjust to a new lifestyle. You'll have moments
where you question if it's even worth it to allocate so much of your
hard earned money towards a loan payment. Don't get deterred
and just remember that this way of life is only temporary and you
have an end in sight. If you choose to live this way for a brief
period of time you'll live a more fulfilled and simpler life down the
road. Envision yourself five, ten, or fifteen years from now. You're
living a debt-free life and your paycheck is no longer going

towards thousands of dollars in loans and growing interest. You've beaten the odds and changed your life and your family's future. Having the knowledge and the skills to live a life within your means is game-changing. You've set the course for the rest of the people around you and have given them hope that they can live a life just like you.

Where We Are Now

As I write this book we have officially been debt free for three months. While our day-to-day living has not changed drastically, the relief that I feel each day is something that I wanted to share. I didn't realize how stressed I was about money and every purchase that we made, until we paid that last loan. It is an amazing feeling knowing that every dollar that we make is now ours. Our income before never actually belonged to us; it belonged to our loans. Once you have that mindset that your paycheck is not to be used on what you want, but put directly towards your loans you are on the path to success. Today we get to spend a bit more on groceries (cashews are now in the budget), we get to give more, and we get to enjoy time with each other by doing activities that we may otherwise have passed on. We are currently on "Baby Step #4," *Investing 15% of our income into retirement.* Initially that sounded like a lot of money, but once you find that your paycheck is all yours, your bank account will grow quickly. We recently met with a financial advisor to discuss our options for how to invest and grow our retirement fund. It's important to make sure that your money is not just sitting in a bank account. You need to make calculated decisions when investing your money. Deciding what percentage of your income to invest in a 401k, Roth IRA, or liquidated investments can vary some for everyone. These are some of the more common options and what we have chosen as we start this next chapter of our lives. Yes, we still have a lot to learn and will start to adjust our retirement fund over the next few months to see what works for us. The best part is that we now have the tools to live a life with less worry and more freedom. Don't leave your future to fate. Take the steps to make sure that you too are set up for the rest of your lives by starting your debt free journey today.

What good book doesn't end with a quote and food for thought? I'll leave you with this:

"Your decisions from today forward will affect not only your life, but your entire legacy."

— Dave Ramsey

Quick Reference Guide
for 2 Cent Tips

My 2 Cents #1

Don't get wrapped up in the ease of meals sent to your door, clothes picked out for you, fitness in a box, snacks in a box, dog treats in a box. It's all TOO MUCH!

My 2 Cents #2

Buy when items are on sale and don't buy out of season. You'll spend triple the amount. This applies to food items, not clothing. This is truest when buying fruit and vegetables. You'll start noticing when items are in season because they become heavily discounted. For example, I refuse to buy grapes out of season because they'll cost $7 a bag. When in season, I can get them for half the price. Avocados are another item that can only be purchased in season. If you're spending $2.50 per avocado, then you need to keep reading.

My 2 Cents #3

Stop paying for that $150/month gym membership. I know this one might be hard if you're dedicated to CrossFit, yoga or Orange Theory. I get it, you want to be healthy, but there are other ways for less than $1,800 a year.

My 2 Cents #4

Use the Internet or DVDs to find a killer workout. There are so many great ways aside from paying for a gym membership to still get the same effect.

My 2 Cents #5

When planning a wedding, absolutely make sure you set a budget. If you don't have any budget, you'll spend an exorbitant amount of money and you could end up regretting your purchases. Whether it's $5,000 or $30,000, always set a budget.

My 2 Cents #6

Cancel all those subscriptions that you don't actually need. Magazines, online subscriptions, courses, etc. All of the things that you're paying $9.95 for a month add up quick.

My 2 Cents #7

Eat home as much as possible. You know when you go out and order a glass of wine and realize it's the same price as the full bottle you could've bought? The same is true for everything about your meal out. It's a luxury to eat out but American culture has turned it into our norm.

My 2 Cents #8

Basic cable and internet will save over $1,000 a year. I personally couldn't keep paying $160 a month for cable and internet. Do you watch $40 worth of TV? Probably not, especially if you're working and only home for a couple hours a day like the rest of us. Call them up and find ways to get back to basics.

My 2 Cents #9

Budget for all holidays. Christmas is hard; I get it. Be smart in your purchases and don't go crazy. Buy throughout the year and when you find items on sale. Christmas gifts can be purchased throughout the year, not just within four weeks of the year.

My 2 Cents #10

Never buy bottled water; it's a waste of money and not good for the environment. I know this sounds like you're only saving $2, but think of when you're out and the bottle of water is now $5. Be prepared, always carry your own bottle with you.

My 2 Cents #11

Shop the perimeter of the grocery store. Everything on the outside, including the fruits and vegetables, are the items that are more cost-effective. Did you know a giant bag of carrots costs less than $3? Or that a bushel of bananas costs less than $1.50? Set a challenge and see what you can get your grocery bill down to for two weeks. It will be motivation!

My 2 Cents #12

Go on vacations that don't require a lot of spending. Enjoy and explore the natural scenery. Go to the beach where all you require is a house rental; all of your meals could be made in the house and what more do you need with the ocean out your door? Places that require a lot of spending once you get there are places like Disney and amusement parks. Avoid these places at all cost because once you get there you'll be spending twice as much as your cost to get there.

My 2 Cents #13

Each week, take ten minutes to create your weekly meal plan. Plan out your lunch and dinner with the items you purchased for the week. This will keep your meals creative and allow you to be resourceful when cooking so that no items are wasted.

My 2 Cents #14

Paint your own nails, do your own facials, let your hair be natural. This is an area of sacrifice for women, I know. I couldn't pay someone to do my nails when I could so easily do them myself. Of course, there are certain occasions which warrant the occasional treat. Yes, for my wedding, I did splurge and get my nails done. Otherwise, I went to the hair salon once a year (using a Groupon to find a great deal) and never did I get a facial. The one thing I wanted to do upon being debt free was book a spa day; massage and facial as a treat!

My 2 Cents #15

Learn to change your own oil and do small repairs. Replace your windshield wipers. Be your own car wash. These small tasks will save you a significant amount of money in the long run. Every dollar saved helps!

My 2 Cents #16

Buy your household items in bulk or through a wholesaler. This includes dish soap, hand soap, paper towels, laundry detergent, toilet paper, and tissues. If you want to take it a step further stop buying non-essential paper goods altogether. Save by using real dishes and real hand towels.

My 2 Cents #17

Sell old items in your house that are taking up wasted space. Game changer.

My 2 Cents #18
Avoid shopping. If you don't have self-control just don't go. I followed this practice often. I used to like to wander into stores on the weekend but now I just don't go unless I have a purpose for going.

My 2 Cents #19
Buy generic. Generic food, generic soap, generic hair supplies. They're all the same.

My 2 Cents #20
Stop buying all of the "need it now" gimmicks. Have you heard of the Apple Watch, the Instapot, the Fitbit, and the Apple TV? Of course you have. Don't feel like you need to buy these very expensive items that everyone is raving about. They're not important.

My 2 Cents #21
Stop paying for cable and internet and save over $2,000 a year. Can you cut it out completely? It's easier than you might think and you'll find that you have so much more time.

My 2 Cents #22
Reevaluate your health and car insurance. Is it the best deal that you can get for where you are? Many of the big brand companies cost a premium just for the name. I completely changed my insurance carrier when I found that I was paying the same price and not getting nearly the same amount of coverage as others.

My 2 Cents #23

Don't use convenience stores. Never. Not even for a candy bar or a soda. Just by walking into the store you'll be persuaded to buy items you don't need.

My 2 Cents #24

Use Groupon! Like I said, I always used this app to find hair salons, activities, and even products at Christmas time. Don't get sucked into buying things on here you don't need; stay focused.

My 2 Cents #25

Get outside and do activities. Hiking, running, yoga. These are all free and you can do them right outside your door.

My 2 Cents #26

Eat less meat. Live off of vegetables for a month and you'll notice your grocery bill will be chopped in half.